...ies for Teenagers

...EK LOAN

Cambridge Handbooks for Language Teachers

This is a series of practical guides for teachers of English and other languages. Illustrative examples are usually drawn from the field of English as a foreign or second language, but the ideas and techniques described can equally well be used in the teaching of any language.

Recent titles in this series:

Language Activities for Teenagers

Seth Lindstromberg

PUBLISHED BY THE PRESS SYNDICATE OF THE UNIVERSITY OF CAMBRIDGE
The Pitt Building, Trumpington Street, Cambridge, United Kingdom

CAMBRIDGE UNIVERSITY PRESS
The Edinburgh Building, Cambridge CB2 2RU, UK
40 West 20th Street, New York, NY 10011–4211, USA
477 Williamstown Road, Port Melbourne, VIC 3207, Australia
Ruiz de Alarcón 13, 28014 Madrid, Spain
Dock House, The Waterfront, Cape Town 8001, South Africa

www.cambridge.org

First published 2004
Reprinted 2005

Printed in the United Kingdom at the University Press, Cambridge

Typeface: Adobe Sabon 10/13 pt   *System:* QuarkXPress™   [SE]

A catalogue record for this book is available from the British Library

Library in Congress Cataloging-in-Publication Data

Lindstromberg, Seth, 1949-
    Language activities for teenagers / Seth Lindstromberg.
        p. cm. – (Cambridge handbooks for language teachers)
    Includes bibliographical references and index.
    ISBN 0-521-54193-X (pbk.)
    1. English language – Study and teaching (Secondary) – Foreign speakers – Activity
programs. 2. English language – Study and teaching – Foreign speakers – Activity programs.
3. English language – Study and teaching (Secondary) – Activity programs. I. Title. II. Series.

PE1128.A2L53 2004
428'.0071'2–dc22

                                                                    2003069586

ISBN 0 521 54193 X paperback

Thanks and Acknowledgements

This book, first suggested to me by Jane Clifford, grew out of a collaborative effort involving contributing teachers and editors too – from the beginning, me, and, latterly, Penny Ur as well. I would like to thank everyone whose work has gone into this collection. A glance at the information about the contributors overleaf will reveal how much of it came from them, in particular from Tessa Woodward, Hanna Kryszewska and David A. Hill. I am especially grateful to Tessa for her invaluable comments on the overall shape and content of the book. It was, for example, her idea to include the sections on routines for maintaining order, peer mediation and debating. I would like to express my thanks also to Carla Gardner for her many tips relating to classroom discipline.

The authors and publishers are grateful to the authors, publishers and others who have given permission for the use of copyright material identified in the text. It has not been possible to identify the sources of all the material used and in such cases the publishers would welcome information from copyright owners.

p. 171, 'Love without hope' from *Complete Poems (Robert Graves Programme: Poetry)* Robert Graves, Beryl Graves (Editor), Dunstan Ward (Editor), published by Carcanet Press Limited in 1999; p. 173, 'A Visit to the Asylum' by Edna St Vincent Millay. From *Collected Poems*, HarperCollins. Copyright © 1923, 1951 by Edna St. Vincent Millay and Norma Millay Ellis. All rights reserved. Reprinted by permission of Elizabeth Barnett, literary executor; p. 177, 'There are Big Waves', p. 178, 'Cats sleep anywhere' and p. 188, 'It was long ago' from *Blackbird has Spoken: Selected Poems for Children*, Eleanor Farjeon, Anne Harvey (Editor), published by Macmillan Children's Books in 2000.

Thanks to Lego Company for the use of the brand name LEGO®.

The publisher has used its best endeavours to ensure that the URLs for external websites referred to in this book are correct and active at the time of going to press. However, the publisher has no responsibility for the websites and can make no guarantee that a site will remain live or that the content is or will remain appropriate.

Contributors

Judit Fehér is a freelance teacher and teacher trainer based in Budapest, Hungary. She has taught students at all levels, of all ages and of various nationalities in a wide range of state and private institutions. Activity: 2.2

David A. Hill is a freelance teacher, teacher trainer and materials writer currently based in Budapest. He has worked with English teachers and students of English in more than 20 different countries. He divides his time between writing at home and travelling. He has written teaching materials for Spain, Italy, Singapore, Kazakhstan and China, and two Cambridge University Press readers (*How I Met Myself* and *A Matter of Chance*). He is an associate trainer for NILE, and trains for them in Norwich (UK) every summer. Activities: 3.1, 3.4, 3.6, 3.9, 3.10, 5.2, 5.6, 6.4, 6.5, 6.10, 8.2, 8.6, 9.9

Hanna Kryszewska has taught at the University of Gdansk, Poland, in affiliation with the British Council, since 1979. Since 1991, she has also worked as teacher trainer for Pilgrims Language Courses, UK, and INSETT Poland. She has lectured and led seminars and teacher-training courses in many countries and is co-author of several teachers' resource and teacher-training books and is, as well, a co-author of *Format*, a coursebook for learners aged 16–19. Activities: 3.2, 3.3, 3.5, 3.17, 5.1, 5.4, 5.5, 6.1, 6.3, 6.6, 6.9, 7.1–7.8

Jean Rüdiger-Harper has been teaching teenagers and young adults at St Antonius High School, Appenzell, Switzerland, for the past 14 years and, amazingly, still enjoys her work. She also trains secondary and primary school teachers. Activities: 2.1, 8.12–8.14

Bonnie Tsai is a freelance teacher and trainer. She has been trained in humanistic approaches such as NLP, Psychodramaturgie Linguistique and Suggestopedia. She is associated with Project

Zero at Harvard University, the centre for the application of Multiple Intelligence theory. She works extensively with students of all ages who have learning difficulties arising from a lack of motivation and low self-esteem. Activities: 3.15, 8.3

Tessa Woodward is a teacher, teacher trainer and professional development co-ordinator at Hilderstone College (Kent, UK). She is also the editor of *The Teacher Trainer* journal for Pilgrims (Kent, UK). Her most recent book is *Planning Lessons and Courses* (Cambridge University Press). Activities: 1.1, 1.2, 1.6–1.9, 2.9, 2.10, 3.11, 3.12, 3.14, 3.16, 8.1, 8.7–8.10, 9.4–9.8, 9.10, 9.11

General editor/contributor

Seth Lindstromberg teaches English as a foreign language at Hilderstone College (Kent, England). In this series, he has also edited *The Standby Book*. Activities: 2.3–2.8, 3.7, 3.8, 3.13, 4.1–4.7, 5.3, 5.7–5.9, 6.2, 6.7, 6.8, 7.9–7.11, 8.4, 8.5, 8.11, 8.15, 9.1–9.3

Contents

Introduction

Overview

This collection contains 99 different activities for the classroom. All are described with reference to use in teaching English as an additional language to learners aged 11–16. We have assumed that most users of this book are teachers of English working in *non*-English speaking countries and so have worded the text accordingly. Most, if not all, of these activities can be adapted for use in teaching any foreign language. Many can be used, or adapted for use, with late teens and adults. A few can also be used at primary level.

The activities and your students

Language Activities for Teenagers includes only activities which:

- are of clear learning value for learners aged 11–16
- have good potential to motivate learners in this age group
- are usable in medium-sized classes, and often in classes that are larger.

Many of the activities reflect the current interest within our profession in 'activity-based learning'. Some, as well, involve use of learner-generated ideas and materials. If you would like to become more familiar with these two streams of contemporary methodology, this book is a good place to start.

Principal aims

We aim first of all to offer teachers a reserve of activities that are interesting and useful. In doing this we also especially want to provide support for teachers of:

- classes that are quite mixed in proficiency and interest
- classes which include poorly motivated students
- medium–large classes (i.e. ones numbering up to about 35 or 40)

Mixed classes

Students vary or are similar in many ways – in their interests and plans, in their learning style, in home situation and so on. About all these things one must learn as much as possible concerning the students in each class that one has. Of course, as English teachers, we also need to find out how much English each of our students knows – and what they can do with what they know – and then try to reconcile this information with our syllabuses. There are other things to take into account as well. Whatever we learn about our students or decide about syllabuses and so on, the time comes when we should choose learning activities which are *appropriate*, that is, interesting and useful. Even when a class consists of students who are fairly similar in proficiency and interests, this is not necessarily an easy thing to do. But let us suppose, more realistically, that the members of a class are quite disparate, especially in their interests and in their level of proficiency.

It is also part of being realistic to recognise that among the coursebooks and workbooks available to teachers are many which rely rather heavily on 'closed tasks'. These are tasks which either:

- require a single, particular answer (e.g. most gap fill tasks)

or:

- allow a limited number of answers that are all of about the same level of difficulty (e.g. most reading comprehension questions)

Closed tasks may sometimes serve a useful purpose, especially as test items. But there is a fundamental problem with using them regularly in a mixed class. Specifically, if a closed task is optimally challenging and interesting for some of your students, it is very likely to be too hard, or too easy (and therefore not useful), or not of interest to the rest. For this reason, frequent use of closed tasks is bound to have a negative effect on students' motivation. Of course, you can in principle hand out different closed tasks to different students. But in real life this is not so easy. All of which leaves us with the question, 'For lessons which are consistently interesting and useful for mixed classes, what kind of activities do we need?'

The answer is that we need activities which:

- are flexible in that, for instance, they allow students to choose from a menu of sub-tasks that they can attempt at different levels of ambition
- cater for a variety of learning aims, including ones which have to do with content

Let us look at these two characteristics in more detail.

Giving learners a degree of choice among sub-tasks need not require massive extra preparation on your part. Neither does it automatically require extra preparation to furnish tasks that have a variety of learning aims. Some activities have both flexibility and variety of aims designed into them. Consider the short filler activity 'Kill the text', 2.8 (based on Holme 1991, pp. 60–62).

Kill the text (then bring it back to life)

Age	11 and up
Level	Elementary–Advanced
Time	10–15 minutes
Focus	Accuracy in speech, (optionally) writing, listening to others

Procedure

1 On the board, write a text of 20–40 words, including some vocabulary or grammar that you would like to review.

2 Everyone chooses any two words they wish from the text and writes them down. Add that soon they will need to be ready to use either word in a sentence.

3 Ask if anyone can say a *true statement* (i.e. not a question or command) that includes one of the words they have written down. Make it clear that anonymous statements like *She is happy* are unacceptable but ones like *Annette is happy* are good, provided that Annette is a real person who is really happy. The sentences can be as simple or as complex as the students choose. They should not be connected thematically with the original text.

4 When an acceptable statement has been said *correctly* by a student, erase the word from the board and continue with other words until most or all are gone.

5 If your text is quite short, ask who can say it from memory. Otherwise, ask students to *write* it from memory, individually or in pairs, as they prefer.

(For variations to 'Kill the text' see 2.8, p. 52.)

Comment

• 'Kill the text' is flexible not just because it allows learners to choose from a menu of sub-tasks. (In this case, each word in the text represents a different sub-task.) It is flexible also because the sub-tasks themselves are flexible. That is, once learners have each chosen a word, they can try to form a sentence which is short and simple or they can try to form one which is long and/or syntactically complex and/or expressive of an interesting insight. In other words, the rules of the activity set a minimum requirement (i.e. producing a true sentence which can be extremely short) but leave the door wide open for more ambitious efforts. To generalise, an intrinsically flexible activity has the following characteristics:

– Students should be able to attempt (some part of) the activity at whatever level of difficulty they choose.
– Everyone should have a good opportunity to develop their English in some (but not necessarily the same) way.
– Students have at least some freedom to speak (or write) about themes that are of interest to them.

• The requirement that sentences be well-formed allows you (or other students) to give feedback about the linguistic accuracy of each sentence. Because different students produce different statements, they tend to get different feedback. Therefore, the potential scope of language aims is extremely broad.
• The requirement that sentences be true encourages everyone to try to understand each one, since the truth of a statement can only be determined by considering its content (or message).

All in all, 'Kill the text' is a clear example of an activity which is flexible, has a wide range of language aims and includes a focus on content.

Let us look at another example:

ABC sentences

Age	11 and up
Level	Elementary–Advanced
Time	15–30 minutes
Focus	Accuracy in writing, listening to others

Procedure

1 Ask everyone to write, down the left side of their page, the letters *a*, *b*, *c* and so on up to *j*.
2 Ask them to write sentences according to the following rules:

- The first sentence should, somewhere, contain at least one word beginning with the letter *a*. The second should contain a word beginning with *b*. The third should contain a word beginning with *c*, and so on to *j*.
- Every sentence should be true.
- Everyone should try to write as many sentences as they can (one for each letter) before you say *Stop*.

3 Tell everyone to start writing. Circulate and give 'editorial' tips when you notice language mistakes.

4 Call time when you see that some of your students have written ten sentences and all have written a few. (Ask very early finishers to write extra sentences for the next few letters of the alphabet – as many as they have time for.)

5 Ask students to pair up and instruct them to do as follows: First, Student A *slowly* reads out her sentences to her partner, B. Then she gives B her paper and B stars the sentence he likes best and says why he likes it. Then B reads his sentences to A and she stars the sentence that she likes best and says why.

6 Call the class together and ask a dozen or so students to read out the sentence their partner liked best. Or ask students to form groups of four or so and read their starred sentences to each other.

7 Collect all the papers you did not manage to edit while walking around the class in Step 3. Correct them and hand them back in a later lesson.

(For variations to 'ABC sentences' see 6.2, p. 125.)

Comment

- 'ABC sentences' is intrinsically flexible as follows:
  - There is flexibility as to *amount* of language. A student can do useful work without writing all ten sentences. That is, partial completion is OK. Additionally, there is a straightforward way of getting early finishers to write more than the norm.
  - There is flexibility as to *complexity of language*. Low-proficiency students can write sentences that are short and linguistically simple. Higher-proficiency students can do the opposite.
  - There is flexibility as to *quality of content*. The activity allows both low- and high-proficiency students to express thoughts of any degree of profundity. Indeed, someone almost always writes something that everyone else finds interesting.

- Although (like 'Kill the text') this is potentially an accuracy activity, it also has a strong focus on (non-linguistic) content.

Motivating low-proficiency, poorly motivated students

There are (roughly speaking) four types of low-proficiency student:

1 Some are weak in English because they may have been learning for a shorter time than their classmates; or perhaps they have come from another school where they received insufficient opportunity to progress or did not get enough encouragement. The great majority of students in this group need lots of attention, but they have a good chance of catching up if they get adequate attention.

2 A second group is made up of students with physiological learning disabilities such as poor hearing. This issue is outside the scope of this book.

3 A third group – fortunately not represented in all classes – is made up of children with severe psychological problems resulting, for instance, from traumatic experiences of one kind or another. Dealing with students in this category is also outside the scope of this book.

4 It is a fourth sort of low-proficiency student that most commonly disrupts the work of their classmates and gives teachers headaches. These are students who are weak in English largely because their motivation is low. They attach little importance to all the reasons for learning that we teachers and their better motivated classmates can see: reasons such as gaining knowledge for qualifications and career, experiencing the fascination of discovery, and making one's parents and teachers happy. These poorly motivated students are rarely persuadable by such arguments as *This will all be very useful to you one day*. With such learners it is exceptionally important that your lessons be not just useful (since denial of usefulness may be part of their basic attitude) and well-managed (since this too may be unappreciated) but also interesting and varied. *Language Activities for Teenagers* can help here.

So, what is it, in general, that can make a lesson interesting for 11–16-year olds, even ones with low motivation? Let us look at ten features of interesting lessons, points (a) to (j) below, and then consider an example activity, 'Flash the picture'.

a First, variety is important. A lesson of, say, 50 minutes, should consist of at least three – perhaps four to six – distinct components. In some lessons, these components may be the different stages of a single overall activity which is long but varied. In others, they may belong to two or more separate activities.

b   Activities, and the steps that make them up, should have clearly understood and achievable goals. Ideally, there should also be a tangible or at least observable outcome: a student text, for example, or a performance.

c   Activities with game-like elements are usually very good for generating interest. Such elements include:
   • a degree of competition
   • a goal which is about something other than getting the language right. One example of this kind of goal is identifying as many differences between two pictures as possible within a short time limit; another is solving a brainteaser.

d   A major means of maintaining interest is use of activities which require and encourage students to use the target language for communication of interesting messages.

e   Extensive use of non-language stimuli such as pictures, objects, mime, music and sound effects is crucial if your class includes poorly motivated students.

f   Almost anything you can do to make classwork personally relevant will help. If, for instance, you want students to speak about an object, let it be one that is special to them for some reason – an object, perhaps, that has sentimental value or one they use in connection with a pastime they enjoy.

g   It is always wise to try to discover what topics are of current interest to the age group you are teaching and try to include them, somehow, in your lessons.

h   Periodic opportunity to move about, or at least stand and move, is highly beneficial to students in this age range and can contribute to keeping interest up.

i   Humour is important too. Of course, there is no recipe for this. But, if you create the right sort of atmosphere and show your sense of humour as often as you can, more humour will come from your students. (For more on this, see Medgyes, 2002.)

j   Finally, occasional surprises can help keep students interested and paying attention.

Few activities will include all of these features, but let us look at one that includes several:

Flash the picture

Age	Any
Time	5 minutes
Level	Any (see Variation for beginners, below)
Focus	Nouns and prepositions especially, but other elements of language too, depending on the picture
Material	A large picture on stiff paper or a copy on OHP transparency

Preparation

Choose a picture large enough for everyone to see or copy one onto an OHP transparency. This activity works best with scenes (especially ones that suggest a scenario) which include just a few visually salient people (or things) plus various less salient details.

Procedure

1　Flash or show the picture for a very short time – a second or less.
2　Ask students to say what they saw.
3　Repeat Steps 1 and 2.
4　Show the picture for three or four seconds.
5　Repeat Step 2.
6　Display the picture and keep it in full view. Elicit or teach useful vocabulary and elicit as much comment as you can, for example:
   - facts about what is shown, e.g. If there is a tool, what is it for?
   - speculations about what has just happened or what is going to happen
   - speculations about people's motives for what they are doing
   - interpretations: if the scene is somewhat mysterious or ambiguous
   - solutions: if the scene shows people in a problem situation
   - opinions: if the scene suggests a controversy
   - personal associations, e.g. ask, *Does the picture remind you of anything?*, *Has anyone here ever been in a situation like this?*

(For variations to 'Flash the picture' see 2.3, p. 46.)

Comment (compare with a–j, pp. 6–7)
Among the features that make 'Flash the picture' a potentially interesting activity are:

a　The use of a picture can provide a welcome break from focusing directly on words and texts.
b　The activity has a clear purpose: to revise or teach the vocabulary and grammar needed to talk about a particular picture.

c   The fact that the picture is only flashed (in the beginning) means that anyone who pays close attention has a good chance of noticing something that others will fail to see. Thus, a mood of game-like competition readily develops but, because the activity is brief, it is unlikely to get out of hand.

d   Because different students will notice or think different things about the picture, communication is encouraged. In other words, 'Flash the picture' is communicative because there is an 'information gap' or an 'opinion gap'.

e, f, g   You can choose pictures that relate to topics of current interest to your students.

j   Students may not expect a picture to be used in this way. They may also be surprised by how much they notice during one brief flash.

In addition to choosing activities with potential to be interesting and useful, there are a few additional things one can do in order to help low-level, poorly motivated students to learn:

- Try to *use the truth rule* regularly in small ways. This helps poorly motivated learners to recognise that English can be useful for saying real things here and now.
- Everyone knows that nothing builds motivation like success, so *make your lessons success-oriented*. Design or choose tasks which set everyone achievable aims. In mixed-proficiency classes, flexible activities have a role to play here. One tactic in particular that may get poorly motivated students to perform better is to set very low minimums but then also include an apparently minor requirement which encourages them to exceed the minimum. For example, asking poorly motivated learners to talk in pairs about what they did at the weekend may not work as well as asking one partner to say two *very short* true sentences about their weekend. Their partner should then say *Because . . . ?* at least twice. And the first speaker then has to provide the reasons.

A variation is to set an intriguing frame of some kind that looks small and easy to add something into – either a little or a lot, depending on how much a student can or wants to say. This is often equivalent to designing a core task which is easy for everyone in the class to do, including the weaker students, plus a challenging extra for students who are more proficient.

For example:

Write in the shape

Age	11 and up
Level	Elementary–Advanced
Time	25–45 minutes
Focus	Writing, speaking
Material	Blank sheets of A4 paper

Procedure

1   Hand out the sheets of A4 paper and ask students to draw on it the outline (only the outline!) of an object that is important to them – maybe a gift or souvenir; maybe something they use a lot. Say that their outline should be the size of a hand, bigger if they like. (In higher-level classes, say that the object should almost fill up the sheet.) Explain that they are each going to write some sentences *inside* the outline of their object.

2   Dictate the beginning of the first sentence to be written inside the drawing: *This is . . .* Tell them to finish that sentence and then write some more sentences saying why the object is important to them, when they got it, and so on.

3   After a while, say that anyone who has filled in all the space inside the outline can write more sentences outside their outline if they want.

4   When everyone has written some sentences, students form groups of three to six and read out what they wrote. Say that they can ask questions about each other's objects.

(For variations to 'Write in the shape' see 6.8, p. 136.)

Comment

The outline not only concretises the topic for the students, but says quite clearly that it is not necessary to fill the whole page. Both facts make it relatively easy for students to begin to write.

A final point on the matter of getting students interested is that poorly motivated students are frequently anti-authoritarian in attitude. There are many things you can do to try to create a non-authoritarian mood. Of course, a key way of doing this is to let your sense of humour come out. More generally, as appropriate, try, sometimes, to *be relatively conversational* in tone. This is not the same thing as trying to make your class of teens feel you are one of them (which is usually a really bad idea). It is merely a way of being more human in manner. One example of a concrete step towards achieving this is to try to find alternatives to 'echoing' – the term for when a teacher repeats a student contribution with fairly level or falling intonation, like this:

TEACHER: *Who can tell me a room in a house?*
STUDENT 1:   *Kitchen.*
TEACHER: *Kitchen.*
STUDENT 2:   *Bedroom.*
TEACHER: *Bedroom*, etc.

An easy alternative to echoing acceptable and audible student contributions is to respond in a way that is clear, yet conversational, and which perhaps also invites elaboration: *Yes, I think so too*, *I agree*, *Really?*, *Oh, why?*, *Good point* and so on.

Large classes

There is no use pretending large classes are ideal. All kinds of things become more and more problematic as class size burgeons, e.g. activities which involve movement; oral pairwork and group work (especially in a classroom with hard, echoing surfaces); monitoring any kind of individual and group work; learning about each student as an individual; catering simultaneously to your lowest, highest and average proficiency learners. But some teachers do seem to cope with large classes better than other teachers do. How do they manage this?

Some of their success may come from their personalities. There just *are* people, for instance, who have charismatic, engaging personalities which enable them to capture and hold the interest of large crowds. Although there are ways of becoming more like them – by taking voice and drama lessons or lessons in presentation skills, for example – there tend to be limits on the extent to which people can fundamentally change their personalities. But it should be within the reach of every teacher of large classes to make their job easier by adopting appropriate practices, procedures and techniques. Throughout the book you will find many ideas relevant to managing large classes more successfully. For more on this subject, see Hess (2002) in this series.

Seth Lindstromberg
Kent, England 2003   SethL@hilderstone.ac.uk

1 Maintaining discipline in the classroom

There can be few schools in which teachers are able to take good discipline in the classroom utterly for granted. Usually, in order to establish the kinds of behaviour that are key to a good learning environment, teachers need to invest considerable time, intelligence, patience and planning. Even with such investment, for some teachers – perhaps an increasing number – maintenance of discipline is *the* concern of their working lives. The purpose of this chapter is to suggest practices which might help teachers avoid or overcome a good many difficulties in this area.

It is organised as follows:

- Part one: Basics of maintaining order – 30 key principles
- Part two: Five routines, or repeating procedures, for improving discipline
- Part three: Peer mediation; four procedures that both develop students' English and introduce a method which, through structured reflection and discussion, addresses causes of poor behaviour

Basics of maintaining order

Establishing foundations for orderly behaviour

1 Decide what basic kind of teacher you want to be
   Cowley (2001), who questioned a large number of students, concludes that there are basically two kinds of teachers able to maintain order in a classroom: ones who are firm but fair and ones who are scary. A third kind, teachers who want to be their students' friend, were judged to be poor at controlling their classes and were not well respected. I shall assume below that you want to be a firm-but-fair teacher, not one who is frightening or who tries to curry favour and thereby loses respect.

2 Learn about your school's policies and rules
   Most schools have school-wide rules of behaviour. These may be set out in a booklet given to every teacher and perhaps also to students when they first enrol. Or you may need to ask other teachers informally. In any case, if school-wide rules exist, think about how to make them a basis for your own class rules.

3 In your first lesson, make a list of rules and make them clear
   Devoting part of your first lesson to rules of behaviour makes it less

likely that students will later act unacceptably out of real or feigned ignorance.

4 Get your students involved in framing the class rules

A good basic procedure is to write out a list of suggested rules and bring them to the class as a proposal. Go through the rules one by one inviting suggestions about additions, omissions and rewordings. Invite discussion – especially on the *reasons* for each of the rules. Note down the rules agreed on and bring the final version to the next lesson.

5 Take care with the wording of rules

Gathercoal (1993) points out that rules can often be more effective when they are worded rather generally. He gives the following example (p. 81). A school has a rule saying *No running inside the school*. Some students deliberately walk backwards bumping into people and say that there is no rule against it; they were not running. So a better rule would be something like *Walk safely and considerately in the school*. Besides being both clear and encompassing, this wording has the additional advantage of indicating why the rule exists – to maintain a safe environment. In any case, psychologists tell us that positive wordings, such as *Walk*, tend to be more effective than negative ones, such as *No running*.

6 Consider all key categories of rule

Rules are necessary to protect or maintain the following:

a health and safety, e.g. *Use things in ways that are safe for you and safe for others*

b the property of individuals and of the school, e.g. *We must respect other people's property*, *The only person who should take anything out of a bag is the owner of the bag*

c the rights of others, e.g. *Respect the beliefs and feelings of others*, *We must use polite language*

d the educational process, e.g. *We must help ourselves and others to learn*, *When a student 'has the floor', everyone else should be quiet and listen*, *When the teacher has an announcement or is explaining something, everyone should be quiet and listen.*

Typically, (a)–(c) are covered by all-school rules, leaving (d) as the category for which extra, class-specific rules are needed. However, it may be prudent additionally to consider a 'rule about rules'. For instance, if students feel they do not have to follow the rules until the bell rings or until you manage to get their attention, the onset of every lesson will be delayed. So the following may be a useful rule too: *We follow the class rules from the moment we begin to enter the room until we have left it after being dismissed.*

7 Consider ratifying the rules

Some teachers find it helpful to draw up the final draft of their rules as a contract which they and their students formally sign. An additional option is to ask students each to (1) make a copy of the rules for their parents, (2) sign it, (3) take it home and show it to their parents and (4) bring back a note from their parents saying they have seen the signed rules.

8 Plan the consequences for violations of rules

Many educators recommend making an ordered list of consequences running from light to heavy. If a student has broken a rule, begin by imposing the lightest consequence appropriate for that violation. If the student persists in misbehaving, impose a slightly more severe consequence and so on.

One reason for adopting the 'graded step' method is that, in the case of most infractions, light but definite consequences work better than immediate serious penalties, which are very likely to cause resentment. Among relatively light consequences that you can impose are requiring students to say both how they have misbehaved and what they should in future do instead.

As a medium consequence you might phone a student's parents. And/Or implement the practice of keeping parents informed as follows:

Type up and make multiple copies of a small form with these questions on it:

---

❶ What did I do wrong? ....

❷ Why wasn't my action acceptable? ....

❸ What should I have been doing instead? ....

❹ What will I do in the future? ....

If a student misbehaves, get a copy of the form and go through it with the student. Fill it in according to what the student says. (It might be prudent to get the student to sign it.) Make a copy for your records and mail the original to the student's parents. (This idea comes from an Internet posting by Laraine Reisner at www.nea.org/helpfrom/works4me.)

A heavier consequence might be a 'detention' (i.e. staying after school), especially a detention on a Saturday. Of course, your students must know in advance what the full range of consequences is and it is very wise to inform parents too about your overall approach and about what the range of consequences is.

9 Remind your students of what the rules are

Periodically review the rules. It is especially important to do this during the first two weeks. Doing this *greatly* increases the likelihood that the rules will be followed in the long term.

10 Consider the larger context of rules

Over time, problems are likely to arise if there is a fundamental mismatch between rules set in a school and those which are accepted in the society as a whole. For instance, rules which are made up and enforced in an autocratic manner are likely to engender resentment and friction if the society as a whole is democratic. Nor is it likely that democratic rules will brilliantly succeed in a setting where it is normal for people to accept whatever rules have been set by tradition and authority.

Building on your foundation

1 Learn everyone's name as fast as possible

Knowing your students' names makes a world of difference, particularly if you use their names mostly when giving positive feedback, e.g. *Maarten just gave us a very useful word* or *That was well put, Rita.*

2 Decide who should sit where

Students find it much easier to get seated and settled promptly if you have told them in advance which seat is theirs. Fixed seating also makes it vastly easier for you to learn everyone's name. Finally, if an assigned seat is empty, you can tell immediately who is missing; this means you may not have to use up much time taking attendance. There are a few things to keep in mind when planning who to put where:

- Mixing up boys and girls often helps improve behaviour generally.
- It makes sense to separate students likely to carry on private conversations. (But see 'Friendship pairs', 1.1, for an alternative.)
- The best place for potential trouble-makers is front and centre, as long as they are not all clumped together.
- Students who dislike each other should not have to sit directly next to each other.

3 Plan varied lessons

Many 11- to 16-year olds lack the perseverance and the power of concentration which underlie an ability to finish long tasks all in one go. They tend to be restless, impatient, easily distracted and prone to boredom. Good planning can go a long way towards helping you deal with these predictable tendencies. For a start, you need more tasks for any given lesson with 11- to 16-year olds than you would if you taught older teens or adults. The tasks should be varied too – not just in topic or skill and language focus but in many other ways as well. For instance:

- Focus on different aims at different stages of the lesson.
- Students should sometimes work individually and at other times in pairs or groups.
- From time to time they should try working with new partners.
- Ask them sometimes to work at their desks and at others to stand at the board or move around the room in order, say, to carry out a series of short conversations.
- Balance quiet, study-like tasks with activities that have a game-like character.

(See Woodward (2001) for a comprehensive treatment of lesson planning.)

4 Plan transitions from one task to another

With young learners, you need to bring one task to an end and move on to another swiftly and smoothly as soon as (or better yet, before) you notice the first signs of boredom. Planning can do a lot to help you make these transitions in a confident, competent manner.

5 Give instructions clearly and efficiently

For instructions to be maximally effective they must, first of all, be clear. Also, the fewer instructions you give and the more concise these are, the easier it will be for students to notice and remember them. An added advantage of reducing the number and length of instructions you have to give over the course of a lesson is that this can give students an enhanced feeling that things are running smoothly to an overall plan, and this in turn can do a lot to help them feel more confident about having you as their teacher. ('Spatial anchoring' and 'Temporal anchoring', 1.2, offer two kinds of options for reinforcing the gist of instructions *non*-verbally.)

6 Take predictable concentration trends into account

Many students find it easiest to concentrate during the first 15 or 20 minutes of a lesson so this is often the best time for intensive review or any particularly challenging exercise on new material. Without regular changes of pace, concentration may sag deeply around the middle of a lesson. This could be a good time for a brief spell of movement or music or other respites from sedentary brainwork. Towards the end of a lesson concentration may be trending upwards again. This is a good time to review the challenging material you covered near the beginning of the lesson.

7   Plan how you are going to get everyone's attention while keeping your voice at normal volume
First of all, begin most lessons with an activity that is especially likely to grab your students' attention and get them all looking in the same direction. Hold up an interesting object or photo or direct their attention to a display on your board or OHP screen that is visually interesting (e.g. a picture) or easy to take in (e.g. a short, funny text). You need as well to have a way of bringing your class back together again after any pairwork or group work or indeed after any individual work that your students are likely to do at greatly varying speeds. There are various techniques you can use to make this possible:
- Have on hand a number of noisemakers (e.g. various small bells, chimes and rattles) for use in getting everyone's attention. (If you always use the same one, students may gradually cease to pay any attention to it.)
- Give some instructions and other messages by writing them on the board (e.g. *When you finish, close your books*). Not everyone will notice these messages so, for instance, ring a small bell and, when your students look at you, point to the message.
- Turning out the lights can get a class to stop talking.
- Holding up a sign of a scowling face saying *Shhhhh!* can be effective and also create a little amusement.
- However, techniques such as the ones just mentioned work only if used sparingly. The most reliable tool is, unfortunately, the hardest to describe. Put simply, it is this. You need to be able to *look* like someone who expects students to be quiet and listen as a matter of routine.
Whatever you do, do not shout.

8   Communicate your teaching goals
Make sure your students know what the learning aims of activities are. They are much more likely to stay on task if they know what the task is for. It is especially helpful to spend a bit of time on this when you do an activity of a *new* sort.

9   Create and exploit opportunities for positive acknowledgement
It is a rare student who does not need positive feedback. This can range
from a pleased acknowledgement (*Yes, that's a very good example,
Maite*) to outright praise (*That's a really great story! The ending is
believable but also a complete surprise!*). The how, when and how much
may need to vary quite a bit from student to student. A few prefer a
regular flow of compliments and encouragement that the whole class
can hear. Others are satisfied if it is mainly their best work that is singled
out for a special note or quiet word or two. Positive feedback is
particularly important in the case of students who tend to misbehave
(but not of course when they are actually misbehaving). Some such
students may react best to acknowledgement that you pass on to them
one-to-one outside of class (e.g. *I liked your drawings today. Would you
be willing to draw at the board some time?*).

In general, the most effective feedback tends both to specify what
you liked and to inform the student about its usefulness. For example,
*You have capitalised all the right words. This makes your writing
especially easy for us to read* rather than *Good work* or *Much
improved*.

10   Keep your students fruitfully occupied
Students who have any tendency at all to become unruly are most likely
to do so if they are not on task. Make sure at all times that everyone has
been assigned a useful task (or set of task options) which is within their
level of competence.

11   Be firm, especially in the beginning
One of the easiest ways to lose control of a class is to become known as
someone who is easy to talk:
- out of things such as the enforcement of rules, e.g. rules against
  tardiness
- into doing or allowing things you hadn't planned to, e.g. playing
  another song when you had only planned to play one

As much as you may actually incline towards flexibility about such
things, you may not be in any position to do so until your ability to
maintain control of a class has been demonstrated *over a period of a few
months*. Then you can relax the rules now and then. All this is
summed up in various versions of the old teachers' saying, *Be firm at
the beginning of the year and you will thank yourself near its end.*
(The version I heard first, *Never smile till Easter*, is perhaps a bit
extreme!)

12 Be fair

Early and mid-teens are sometimes sensitive about issues of fairness to a degree that can be quite astonishing. In order to forestall problems in this area, take time now and then to consider whether you are evenly dividing positive feedback and attention generally. For example, during times in a lesson when you call on individual students with questions, do you spend more time relating to some students than others? There are a few things to look out for here. If you pause to ask questions while writing on the board, it may be that you generally stand at the same side of the board slightly turned towards it. This may mean that at such times you always look more at one side of your class than at the other. Or, like many teachers, you may find that your attention gravitates towards your most vocal students, or towards the ones who are best at making eye contact, or (it is possible!) towards a student you find unconsciously appealing because he or she reminds you of someone else. And beware of tendencies or impressions which cause you to divert attention *away from* particular students. For instance, it is risky to make assumptions of this sort: *Kazuo looks like he just wants to be left alone so I won't put him under any pressure.* My experience suggests that students are not so easy to figure out just from how they look and that ones who seem to have a 'don't bother me' demeanour are as likely as anyone else to feel bad if they get less attention than the rest. In fact, so easy is it to be misled by impressions or just to overlook things in this area that it is a very good idea from time to time simply to ask students one-to-one, *Do you think I am treating you fairly?*

13 Answer questions clearly and respectfully

Asking a teacher a sincere question is seen as a risk by many students. So much depends on the teacher's reaction. A reply that seems dismissive, perfunctory or unclear can have a powerful, negative effect on a student's attitude. If you do not know an answer, admit it. Try, though, to find out so you can answer in a later lesson.

14 Use the whole room

Lay claim to the whole room. Go everywhere you can as often as you can, especially (but not just) during pairwork and group work. Look at what students are writing. Speak to everyone individually *at close range* as often as is feasible given the size of your class. Once in a while be surprising; go to the back of the room and call on someone at the front, and so on. But in general, move *towards* anyone causing trouble rather than away from them. To do the latter only teaches them that they can get rid of you by misbehaving. (For more on use of the room see p. 23.)

15 Try to learn about how you come across to your students
Reflect on your verbal and non-verbal behaviour. Teachers sometimes have unconscious habits that distract or irritate their students – and teenagers can be very intolerant of these! Perhaps ask a close colleague to sit in on a lesson or two and afterwards tell you if they have noticed anything. Or video yourself once in a while. Even a sound recording can be helpful (and unobtrusive to make). I, for instance, had 23 years of teaching behind me before a couple of other teachers brought it to my attention that I have spells of saying *Uhh* with irritating frequency.

16 Avoid sarcasm
Teachers who use sarcasm tend to ruin all hope of working constructively with any student they turn it on. If a truant has finally come to class, a comment like *Oh, look who's finally decided to come to class!* is only likely to breed resentment and encourage further truancy. Rather, react in a way that has some chance of making the student easier rather than harder to deal with in future – something like, for instance, a cheery *Hello, Kim!*

17 Be punctual yourself and expect punctuality from your students
Hopefully, your school has rules about lateness and procedures for dealing with infractions. Whether or not it does, there are a few other measures you can take on your own to encourage students to come on time:

- The most important thing of all is to start teaching at the very beginning of the lesson period. It only encourages students to come late if you delay the onset of a lesson while latecomers get settled down. The first minutes of a lesson are those during which students are generally most alert. These minutes should not be wasted by you or anyone else!

- When presenting your seating plan to the class, tell them that habitual latecomers will be moved to the front of the class. If latecomers stop coming late, consider moving them to some part of the class they might like better – but make it clear to them that renewed tardiness will get them moved right back to the front of the class.

- Take attendance in such a way that students who are late see you making a note of their tardiness.

- Insist latecomers stay a minute or two after class and explain to you why they were late. Keep a record of latecomers' explanations;

perhaps ask the latecomers themselves to write time of arrival and reason into a 'late-book'.

- When a latecomer arrives, immediately call him or her to the front of the class to do some such prominent job as write some of your boardwork for you. (But *never* openly describe this as punishment since you do not want to discourage these students from coming to class at all!) My experience is that few inveterate latecomers like to find themselves in the spotlight like this as soon as they walk into the room.

18 Keep your temper at all costs

Do not take things too personally. When teenagers are rude to you or about you, it is most likely because you represent authority in general. Besides, few people have a perfect understanding of the norms of civility by the time they are 15 or 16, let alone 11. When a student has said something that is out of order or things seem to be about to get tense for any reason, it may be best to make a humorous remark, to change the subject or move on to a new activity. If you do feel you have to comment directly on unacceptable behaviour, try to bear in mind that negatively worded commands can trigger automatic negative denials (e.g. TEACHER: *Please don't talk while I am.* STUDENT: *I wasn't talking!*) unlike a positively worded equivalent (e.g. TEACHER: *Please pay attention so you can do the next activity.* STUDENT: *I was.* TEACHER: *Good then.*).

19 If you get into confrontations, provide students with face-saving solutions

- Offer them at least one solution which is not only satisfactory to you but which is one they can accept without loss of face. This is especially vital if other students are watching and listening.
- Talk in terms of unacceptable *behaviour*; make every effort to avoid making students feel, or giving them a chance to claim, that you are telling them off because you just do not like them as a person. Otherwise, the student may feel (as some appear all too willing to feel or to claim) that it does not matter much how they behave – they are going to get into trouble anyway.
- Focus on the future. Do not get involved in seeking to establish exactly what did or did not happen yesterday or a few minutes ago. Try to find ways to make things happen better in the future. Wordings such as the following might be useful: *OK, next time let's . . .* or *How can we avoid this problem next time?*
- Zealously avoid getting drawn into any heated exchanges with individual students in front of the whole class. If need be, have

private talks with anyone who is really upset or wildly unreasonable, in the corridor during class or somewhere private after class. In the latter case, do not put the meeting off for too long or you may lose credibility.

20 Involve the parents
In cases of repeated and/or serious misbehaviour, you *must* attempt to get the support, or at least the understanding, of the parents. Success comes most easily here if:

- you make contact with all parents as soon as a course begins (or even before) and do what you can to keep parents informed about how their children are participating as the course goes along
- you report instances of *good* behaviour too

Routines for improving discipline

The following five procedures are ones which teachers can make a part of *every lesson* to help create an orderly learning environment.

1.1 Jobs for friendship pairs and very useful persons

Age	7 and up
Level	Any

These two routines both involve deputising particular students to carry out specific support functions in the classroom.

Friendship pairs

Students – particularly girls – are likely to have a friend in the same class who they will want to sit next to. These pairs of friends may wear similar clothes and exhibit various other kinds of bonding behaviour. Accept and capitalise on these 'friendship pairs' (provided the students behave when together) by assigning particular responsibilities to them. For example, each pair can be responsible for a different one of the following tasks:

- cleaning the board
- putting dictionaries and coursebooks back on shelves
- clearing up litter
- checking bulletin boards to make sure things are up-to-date
- writing five test questions on the day's vocabulary (to be put to classmates at the beginning of the next lesson)
- transforming certain bits of boardwork into posters for display on a wall

Very useful persons

There will also be students (girls as well as boys) who do not appear to have a best friend. It is very important to include these students too and to use an equally positive role name ('friendship pairs' was the first) such as 'very useful person' (VUP). Different VUPs each take on a task from the list below on a fixed or rotating basis:

- check attendance
- pass out handouts
- pin things up
- put resources back in boxes
- warn you when it is five minutes before the end of class
- draw things on the board
- tell simple jokes (which you can give them if necessary)
- lead brief physical exercise breaks (e.g. call out *Stand up. Stretch. Lean left.*)

Create 'revolving tasks' which can be done by different friendship pairs or VUPs in different lessons. For example, they can take turns writing up the main points of each lesson in a notebook kept especially for this purpose. This task is made easier if, at the end of each lesson, you elicit from the class 'what was done', 'how it was done' and 'why'.

Tessa Woodward

1.2 Spatial anchoring

Age	Any
Level	Any

This category of routines is about being consistent in how you use particular areas of your classroom in order to help students more readily understand what they are supposed to do. Being consistent in the ways described below may mean you can make your instructions more succinct and that you need to repeat the same instructions less often.

Example routines

Sectoring boardwork

Be consistent about where you put what kind of material on the board or walls. For example, use the top left-hand corner of the board for vocabulary and the top right for instructions and reminders. If you *are* consistent, just moving toward that area can prepare your students for what you are going to do.

Sectoring the room

Use different parts of the classroom for doing different things. For instance:

- stand in a particular spot when you want either to get everyone's attention or to administer light, general disciplining
- from another spot, give instructions
- from another make announcements relating to school affairs

After a while, you may only have to walk towards the attention-getting spot to cause students to begin to break off what they were doing. And when you stand in your 'instruction spot' (for instance), students will automatically know what class of information you are giving them. Give *positive* feedback from everywhere else!

Variation

Effects similar to those of 'spatial anchoring' can be achieved by setting aside particular parts of a lesson period for particular kinds of work. One reason for this is that many students seem to find it difficult to profit from an activity in any way unless and until they are able to mentally assign it to a familiar category such as 'review', 'quiz', 'learning grammar', 'game', 'conversation with a partner', 'whole class discussion'. Temporal anchoring is one way of helping these learners categorise activities quickly and thus find it easier to settle down and get on with the task. The need for consistency in the ordering of lesson stages tends to be greatest: in large classes, with immature learners, and with learners who find it difficult to concentrate.

Acknowledgement

See Grinder and Doone (1991) for more on spatial anchoring and other useful frameworks and practices deriving from the branch of applied psychology known as Neuro-Linguistic Programming.

Tessa Woodward

1.3 Noise control: the disappearing word

Age	7–15
Level	Any

Noise control is a major problem for some teachers. Here is an idea which may help you to keep students quiet when they should be quiet in a relatively light-handed fashion.

Procedure

1 At the beginning of every lesson, write a word or short phrase on the board.
2 Every time you have to remind the entire class to be quiet, rub out a letter, starting from the end of the word.
3 If the word has not disappeared when the lesson is over, everything is OK. If all (or most) of the whole word has survived, the class gets a reward. If the word completely disappears, impose a negative consequence.

Tip

Choose a word or phrase that you want to review. Given the amount of attention that is likely to be paid to it, the chances are pretty good that a lot of your students might remember it for the future!

Acknowledgement

- This idea has been adapted from an Internet posting from Deborah Allen.
- Internet bulletin boards are, incidentally, a good source of ideas for discipline routines. This routine, and the two which follow (1.4 and 1.5) come from the following Internet URL of the National Education Association (USA): www.nea.org

1.4 Confiscating things

Age	6–15
Level	Any
Material	A suitable box and something to decorate it with

Sometimes students bring in things and distract themselves and others by showing them off or playing with them. Here is a way of confiscating small objects in a way that minimises resentment.

Preparation

1 Find a box big enough to contain what you are likely to put in it.
2 Decorate it and label it something like *Room 10 safekeeping box*.

Procedure

1 Show your class the box and say that this is where students have to put objects they do not stop playing with.

2   Enforce the 'safekeeping box' rule whenever students ignore a request to stop playing with an object or showing one off.

Tips

- Always assure students that they can retrieve their objects at the end of the lesson.
- Speak of the box as belonging to the room or the class rather than to you.
- Mention that anyone who finds it difficult to stop playing with something can put it in the box voluntarily.
- If something won't fit *in* the box, put it under or near the box.

Acknowledgement

This routine has been slightly adapted from an idea posted on the Internet by Heather Greenwood at a NEA (US National Education Association) teachers' tips website.

1.5 Behaviour charts

Age	Any
Level	Any

When writing reports or discussing students with parents, it makes all the difference if you can buttress your comments by citing actual events and homework assignments. Being able to do so increases your credibility and this reduces the likelihood of argument. The following procedure enables you to keep note of what you observe about your students from lesson to lesson in a usefully detailed fashion.

Preparation

1   Create a very short abbreviation or code for all the common types of behaviour, good and bad, e.g.

NS = Had all **N**ecessary **S**tuff (pencils, etc.) today

2   On the largest size of photocopy paper you can use, make a seating chart with the largest possible box for each name. Write each name fairly small so that, inside the box, there is room around the name for brief notes. (Perhaps put the front and back halves of the seating chart on separate sides of your sheet.)

3   Make multiple copies of your chart – one for each week or so, depending on how often this class meets and how long the lesson periods are.

Procedure

As often as you can, record incidents and behaviours that are significant for particular students. For example:

- For a troubled or troublesome student, note cases of improvement and backsliding on a lesson-by-lesson basis.
- For students who are generally well-behaved, make summing-up notes about especially good behaviour on a weekly basis.

Example codes

H	= Homework done
OnT	= On Task
OfT	= Off Task
"	= same again today
noP/N	= No Pen(cil)/Notebook

Acknowledgement

This is a slight expansion of an idea posted on the Internet by Melanie McCarty at a NEA (US National Education Association) teachers' tips website.

Peer mediation: structured discussion of conflictual behaviour

Up to now, this chapter has mainly been about how teachers can promote orderly behaviour in their classes and deal with behaviour that is unacceptable. We now turn to peer mediation, which is, in its full form, a way of involving learners in the resolution of conflicts arising from such behaviours as name-calling, rumour-mongering and physical intimidation. In the foreign language class, peer mediation – *even in the introductory phase presented here* – serves the additional purpose of developing a wide range of communication skills, particularly ones to do with fruitful discussion.

The peer mediation (PM) process involves:

- two people in dispute (i.e. two 'disputants')
- a neutral fellow student or students acting as mediator(s)
- one or more 'observers'

It can begin when the participants state that they will:

- agree that there is a conflict
- accept mediation

- try to identify and solve the problem at hand
- be respectful of others
- tell the truth
- work constructively
- listen without interrupting
- take responsibility for implementing any agreement that is reached by all the parties together

When applied to a specific conflict, the immediate aim of PM is not to find out who is right or wrong but to come up with a workable solution. An important long-term social aim of giving students hands-on experience in PM is to help them learn how to get along with people generally.

The following four activities (1.6–1.9) show how peer mediation can be introduced stage by stage over a number of lessons with the final activity (1.9 'Dry run') being a complete PM simulation. This suite of activities stops just short of implementation of PM to resolve real conflicts between students in your class. If you wish to take this final step, there are numerous excellent PM websites you should investigate before you do.

Whether or not the concern is with conflicts that have actually arisen in your class, with ones that individual students have been involved in elsewhere, or with ones that students merely hear or read about, doing PM in English has good potential to help learners develop their communicative competence in a variety of aspects. Because every member of a class eventually takes on each of the three key roles (disputant, mediator and observer), each gets structured experience in all of the following:

- listening, speaking, reading and writing for definite purposes (At one time or another, all four skills are brought into play.)
- note taking (e.g. Mediators should take notes.)
- summary writing (e.g. Mediators may write summaries.)
- explaining clearly what happened (e.g. Disputants must tell their stories and mediators may orally summarise them.)
- agreeing, disagreeing, discussing (All of these things happen in a PM session.)
- preparing questions (e.g. Mediators do this after listening to the disputants' stories.)
- empathetic thinking (e.g. Disputants are asked to imagine themselves in another's position.)
- objectively considering one's own acts, motivations and justifications

from another's point of view (e.g. As a result of hearing another student take one's own role and speak about what was done and why.)

- brainstorming solutions (e.g. In the search for solutions to a dispute.)
- producing written agreements (e.g. Near the end of a PM process.)

Finally, if you have ever wondered how to exploit such material as agony aunt columns, there can be few better ways than doing introductory PM.

1.6 Writing scenarios

Age	15 and up
Level	Lower-intermediate–Advanced
Time	30–45 minutes
Focus	Reading, listening, discussing, scenario writing, awareness of emotional tone, giving balanced accounts of conflicts
Material	One or two: (a) short audio or video excerpts or (b) reading texts on OHP transparencies or photocopied (you need class sets), (optional) a strip of OHP transparency for each group of three students

This activity develops students' ability to pare stories down to the key facts, clearly ordered.

Preparation
Scan print resources such as agony aunt (i.e. personal advice) columns and/or listen to soap operas and pick out a story of a fairly minor conflict between two people. In a low-level class these materials may be partly or wholly in the mother tongue.

Procedure
1 Explain to the class that over the next few weeks you will be teaching them a way of solving conflicts and that if they like what they learn, they can use it for the rest of their lives. Explain that the first step will be understanding a conflict and writing it up as a scenario, a kind of mini-story.
2 Show the letter to the class (or play the soap extract).
3 Through elicitation with the whole class, transform the gist of the conflict into a scenario of between 10 and 20 lines and write it on the board. (See the example letter and scenario on page 31.)

The scenario should include:
- a summary of what happened to cause the conflict
- the perspective of each of the two parties
- some comment on how the two people feel and why

Additionally, the scenario should be more balanced and (probably) cooler and more factual than the portrayal of the conflict in the original material.

As you build a scenario through elicitation, point out other typical features of a scenario. For example:

a   Sentences in a scenario tend to be fairly short and simple.

b   Scenarios are written in the third person.

c   Scenario writers often write as if they know what others think and feel.

d   Scenarios are written mainly in the present simple tense.

e   Scenarios present events and situations in the order they happened.

(Feature (d) invites us to think the happenings are of interest to us here and now; features (d) and (e) invite us to think about what happens next.)

4   Form groups of three and give each a short text (such as the 'Dear Jenny' letter on page 31) which is about a conflict which might be found in a magazine for teenagers. Give them time to read it, discuss it and write a scenario in English from it.

5   One by one groups show or read out their scenarios. In whole class discussion bring out the strong points of each so as to reinforce the guidelines above on the structure and tone of a good scenario.

Follow on

In later lessons, ask students to find materials of their own (e.g. in newspapers) which they then transform into scenarios. Students can work on the same text or on different texts. Students read out or show their scenario to others. Finally, students draw on their own life experience to write scenarios which they then read out to each other.

Tip

Step 4: If each group writes its scenario on a strip of OHP (overhead projector) transparency, these can be displayed via OHP in Step 5.

Variation

At Step 4, give different students texts of different difficulty. Students with quite low-proficiency texts can have texts partly in the mother tongue.

EXAMPLE

Agony Aunt letter

Dear Jenny,

My name is Larry Smith and I have this friend and I really like him but he always changes some part of my name so it sounds ridiculous. Some days he calls me 'Scary' or 'Scary Larry' and then he also calls me 'Smiff' or 'Sniff' or 'Scary Larry Sniff'. I wouldn't mind so much if he only did it in private, but he does it especially when there are other kids around. I told him to stop but he wouldn't. He thinks his names for me are hilarious and says I should have more of a sense of humour. Now other kids have started to call me the same things, even the girls. He's turned into a real pain. I lost my temper with him the other day and told him he was a XXXXX. We almost had a fight. I don't want him to be my enemy. What should I do?

Larry

© CAMBRIDGE UNIVERSITY PRESS 2004

Scenario

Larry Smith has a friend. This friend thinks it is funny to call Larry 'Scary Larry' and other similar things. Larry asks his friend to stop doing this but his friend refuses. Larry thinks his friend is being disrespectful to him. The friend thinks Larry is too serious about this. Other kids start to call Larry funny names. Larry's pride is hurt. So he insults his friend. They quarrel and almost fight. Larry is not happy now and wonders what to do. His friend wonders why Larry became so nasty the other day.

© CAMBRIDGE UNIVERSITY PRESS 2004

Tessa Woodward

1.7 Discussing ground rules

Age	15 and up
Level	Lower-intermediate–Advanced
Time	20–30 minutes
Focus	Discussion, thinking about minimum acceptable behaviour during discussions
Material	A class set of blank index cards (optional) a class set of photocopies of the ground rules or the same on an OHP transparency (see below), a large sheet of poster paper for the final version of the rules

This activity introduces students to important rules about behaviour during peer mediation sessions.

Example beginning for intermediate level – Ground rules

In peer mediation people in conflict take turns telling mediators what happened. There is then time for questions, role plays, brainstorming and discussion. Sometimes emotions run high so we need ground rules to make sure things stay peaceful and positive during the discussion. In your group discuss the following rules and add more if you can:

a   Everybody must stay seated during the mediation.

b   Disputants try not to exaggerate.

c   Disputants say how they would like to solve the conflict.

d   Nobody should interrupt while another person is speaking.

e

f

g

h

Preparation

Photocopy a class set of the beginning of a 'ground rules' handout (or write the beginning on the board or an OHP transparency). Ideally, you will be able to elicit from your students the items following your initial list of rules. For instance, if you used the beginning just below, you would aim to elicit rules from (e) on.

Procedure

1 Put students into groups of about four, distribute your ground rules handouts and allow time for discussion within the teams.

2 In plenary, ask if anybody has any more rules to add. If students say sensible things such as *No shouting* or *No touching*, tell everyone to add them onto their ground rules handout. It is important that everyone agrees that all the rules make sense.

3 Explain that you will produce a poster showing all the rules and that they will be using them in a later lesson.

OTHER USEFUL RULES

Be polite (e.g. no insults or name calling). ....

Remember that there is a problem to solve. ....

Help those who are trying to solve it. ....

Tell the truth. ....

Tip
Add that other rules might be added later, if necessary.

Tessa Woodward

1.8 Asking questions about people's stories and thinking of solutions

Age	15 and up
Level	Lower-intermediate–Advanced
Time	45 minutes
Focus	Reading, listening, making notes in categories, preparing questions, discussion
Material	A class set of photocopies, a written scenario (example on p. 35), a notebook for everyone

Here students gain experience in listening to and taking notes on disputants' stories, asking disputants about these stories and brainstorming suggestions about how a conflict might be resolved.

Preparation

Prepare a class set of copies of a scenario. (See the example on p. 35.)

Procedure

1 Explain that during peer mediation anybody who is not actually speaking at the time will be taking notes on the story being told by one of the disputants. Add that this is very important but that it takes practice to listen to someone's story and simultaneously take notes on it and so this is what they are going to practise now.

2 Hand out a short scenario relating to a minor, imaginary disagreement between two members of staff at a school. (See the scenario on p. 35.)

3 Check that everyone understands the scenario.

4 Ask everyone to make three sections in their notebooks: one entitled *I agree*, one *I disagree* and one *Questions I want to ask*.

5 Explain first that *you* will be playing the role of Ms Parker and will tell the story from her point of view and second that, while listening, they should write notes on the things they agree with (or think are reasonable) and disagree with (or think are unreasonable) about her story.

6 Pretend to be Ms Parker. (See the first role card, on p. 35.) On the board, write a *D* for disputant (or hold up a sheet of paper with a *D* on it) and tell the story in the first person, emphasising how you were in no way at fault and blaming Mr Bumble as much as possible. Say how you would like the problem to be resolved. Be natural but pause between points so that everyone has time to write things down.

7 Move away from the *D* on the board (or put down your *D* sheet). In either case, stand in a different place to underscore the fact that you are now out of role.

8 Ask them to look at their notes about what they agreed and disagreed with and use them to write in their notebooks questions they would like to ask Ms Parker. Circulate and help with wording.

9 Move back to where 'Ms Parker' was standing and again pretend to be her. Ask them for their questions (and answer them).

10 Repeat Steps 6–9 as Mr Bumble. (See the second role card, on p. 36.)

11 In pairs, students voice any ideas they have about how Ms Parker and Mr Bumble can resolve their dispute.

12 Bring the class together and ask pairs to tell the rest of the class any suggestions they have thought of.

EXAMPLE

Scenario

A school has only ten parking spaces. There are eleven teachers with cars. When Mr Bumble arrived late on Monday morning, all spaces were filled. He parked behind Ms Parker's car. When she left school early to go to the dentist, she found her car blocked in by Mr Bumble's car. She tried to find Mr Bumble, but he had taken his class to the local library. Furious, she phoned for a taxi and the following day left an angry note on Mr Bumble's desk demanding that he pay for her taxi. She is very upset. He read the note and is now very upset too because he had left his car keys with the school secretary in case anybody needed to move his car. He is very angry about the tone of her note and he does not intend to pay for her taxi. He wrote an angry note saying all this and put it on her desk. Both Mr Bumble and Ms Parker complained about each other to a mutual friend who suggested they seek mediation.

© Cambridge University Press 2004

Note

See the two role cards that follow, which will help you think of what to say when role-playing the two disputants.

Role card 1, for Ms Parker

You are a teacher at a school. You go to school by car every day and go early to find a parking spot. You park carefully. You like most people on the staff but find Mr Bumble very disorganised. On Monday you arrived at school early and parked near the entrance to the car park because you wanted to leave early that day to go to the dentist's. When you left class to get in your car, you found you were blocked in by another car – Mr Bumble's! You went to his classroom to find him but it was empty. Furious, you went to the office to call for a taxi. When it arrived, you went to the dentist's but were so late you missed your appointment. Now you have a bad toothache. You wrote an angry letter to Mr Bumble. You feel he should pay for the taxi, apologise and promise to park more carefully in future.

© Cambridge University Press 2004

Role card for 2, Mr Bumble

You are a teacher. You go by car to school every day. Because you often arrive later than the other teachers, you often find no parking space. You usually have to spend ten minutes or so looking for a space in the street. On Monday, you could find no spaces in the street and, worried about being late for class, you parked behind another car. You left your keys with the school secretary in case anybody needed to move your car. The next day, you found an angry note on your desk, from Ms Parker. She demanded money from you. You are very angry because the letter was not very nice and you feel you had no choice about where to park. You think the school should make more parking spaces and that anybody who double-parks should leave their keys with the school secretary. You think this is perfectly sensible.

Tessa Woodward

1.9 Dry run, with role reversal and solutions brainstorm

Age	15 and up
Level	Lower-intermediate–Advanced
Time	50–70 minutes (can be done over two lessons)
Focus	Speaking, listening intently and remembering what has been said, role-switching, a little reading
Material	Large index cards or sheets of blank paper, the ground rules poster (from 1.7), copies of a scenario, role cards and instructions for observers (see p. 38), a notebook for each learner, a sheet of paper for each mediator on which to write the agreement

This complete peer mediation simulation can be done in two lessons if you break somewhere in the middle (e.g. after Step 11). Just make sure everyone brings their materials and/or notes to the lesson that follows.

Preparation

1   Prepare the right number of role cards for disputants and instruction cards for mediators and observers (for Step 6).
2   You also need your ground rules poster as well as three large index cards or sheets of blank paper for each mediation group and an additional sheet of blank paper for the mediator(s) in each group.

Procedure

1   Divide the class into mediation groups, or 'teams'. With a small class, the minimum you need for a team is two people in conflict (the 'disputants'), one mediator and one observer. With large classes, form teams of six, each comprising two disputants, two mediators and two observers.

2   The mediators sit opposite the disputants with the observers (or both observers) sitting at either the left or right side of the table. The result is participants sitting on three (not four) sides of a table.

D D

☐ O

M

3   Hand out index cards and ask students to write on them, as appropriate to their role, either a huge *M* (= mediator), *O* (= observer) or *D* (= disputant). Each participant then lays their card face up on the table so that the others can see it.

4   Display your ground rules poster and review the rules.

5   Give everyone a copy of the scenario and allow time for them to read it.

Scenario

Sue and Keiko are classmates. Sue asks to borrow Keiko's dictionary for the weekend for some extra homework she has to do. Keiko agrees. On Monday Sue brings the dictionary back, in a plastic bag. Later when Keiko looks at the dictionary carefully, she sees that it is rather battered, has juice stains on some pages, and other pages are torn or missing. She feels angry. She thinks Sue should have apologised and offered to buy her a new dictionary. She stops speaking to Sue. Sue tries to talk to Keiko, but Keiko simply turns and walks away. Sue is hurt and upset.

© CAMBRIDGE UNIVERSITY PRESS 2004

---

6   Give the disputants their role cards and the observers their instruction cards.

Role card for Sue

You are an easy-going student with lots of brothers and sisters. You don't have many things of your own at home and your brothers and sisters often borrow your things. You want to do well at school. You admire Keiko who is a good student. You want to be her friend. You borrowed her dictionary for the weekend. You brought it back promptly. Now Keiko won't talk to you and you don't know why.

Role card for Keiko

You are a hard-working student and an only child. You want to make friends at school. You are very careful with your things. You lent your dictionary to a friendly classmate named Sue. She brought it back on time, but when you looked at it carefully, it was torn and dirty, and some pages were missing. You want Sue to apologise and to buy you a new dictionary. You would like to be friends, but you think that Sue's attitude to your property has been careless and disrespectful.

Instructions for observers

Everybody in peer mediation has a different job. As an observer, you do not have to talk at all but you do have to watch, listen carefully and make notes on the following:

- Does everybody stick to the ground rules?
- Does everybody do the steps of the mediation in the correct order?
- Do the disputants say how they feel and what they want?
- Do they think of solutions to the problem?
- Does the mediator offer useful solutions?
- Is agreement reached?
- Is it written down?

7   Explain that, using their role cards, disputants take it in turns to say what they think happened, how they feel about it and what they think should happen next. Add that while each disputant is speaking, the mediators and the other disputants note down in their notebooks points of agreement and disagreement between the two disputants. Explain that the disputants will have to listen to each other *extremely carefully* because, after both have spoken, they will switch roles and then tell the other person's side of the story *from that person's point of view*. To do this, they will need to take into account what this other disputant has recently said (in Steps 8 and 9).

8   In each team, the mediators flip a coin to see which disputant goes first.

9   When the first disputant has finished speaking, everybody except the observer(s) can ask clarification questions. This step is then repeated with the second disputant.

10   After both disputants have spoken, the mediators state which things both parties seem to agree on and which things they disagree on. The disputants say whether this summary is accurate or not and, if not, they offer corrections.

11   The disputants swap seats *and* points of view and, in turn, each now says what happened from the point of view of the disputant in whose seat they are now sitting.

12   In each group, the mediator asks the disputants each to write a list of ideas for solving the problem. They should write quickly and not worry about whether the ideas are possible or practicable. If necessary, the mediators help disputants to think of and formulate ideas.

13   The mediator asks the disputants to discuss each other's ideas. The mediator can prompt the discussion by commenting on (im)practicality and the effect of each idea on the different parties or on others mentioned in the scenario. The idea is to arrive at a mutually agreeable solution.

14   Once the disputants have agreed on a number of components of a solution, they should dictate these to the mediator who makes sure that the agreement includes details about the who, what, where, when and how of the proposed actions. Disputants sign the agreement.

15   This is the end of the mediation itself. Now it is the turn of the observers to comment on the overall behaviour of their team. This will help the teams to evaluate themselves and suggest improvements to the process, the rules and their own behaviour.

16 Bring the class together and ask disputants how they felt about the experience of playing a role and then switching roles. It may be, for instance, that some will say they now have a better understanding of each side in the dispute. If so, introduce the word *empathy* and elicit comment on its meaning and importance in conflict resolution.

Follow on

Many different kinds of writing are possible following a peer mediation, for example:

- They each write a newspaper article about the dispute or a 'what happened next' story.
- Students gather conflict stories which are of more personal relevance and rewrite them as scenarios. The results can be used in future peer mediation sessions.

Variation

Step 7: Ask observers to make notes on the quality of others' English. For example, you might ask them to monitor the verbs used by disputants when they tell their stories (past simple forms should predominate), suggestion-expressions used during the brainstorm (e.g. *They could both . . .*) and second conditionals during the ensuing discussion of the practicality of the solutions collected during the brainstorm.

Tip

If you have any extra low-proficiency students, give them the role of observer or that of mediator in tandem with a student whose proficiency is significantly better.

Comment

- Once students know how to do peer mediation, they can use it in or out of class to solve their own disputes. There are two vital conditions, however:
  a Participation in such sessions must be *entirely voluntary*.
  b The disputes concerned must be fairly minor; peer mediation of this kind is not appropriate, for example, in cases where one student has physically attacked another.
- A cadre of practised peer mediators can be formed by giving student-volunteers extra-curricular training. Any two students who agree to participate as disputants choose a mediator from this cadre.

Acknowledgements
Thanks to my niece Clare Hogan for telling me about her experience as a
peer mediator in her school. I have also drawn on Johnson and Johnson
(1996) and Swift (2000).

Tessa Woodward

2 Short, auxiliary activities: ice-breakers, warm ups, breaks and closers

Each activity in this chapter can play one or more of the following roles in a lesson:

- ice-breaker
- warm up
- break
- closer

A few can also serve as lead-ins to longer, main-lesson activities.

Let us look at the first four functions in more detail.

An *'ice-breaker'* is a short activity specifically for use with learners who do not yet know each other well. The most obvious purposes of an ice-breaker are to help people learn each other's names and to help students begin to get acquainted with each other. A typical ice-breaker will also fulfil most of the aims of a warm up, break and/or closer (see further below). Finally, an ice-breaker will generally enable you to see each student in action – if only briefly – before you embark on other work. This can be invaluable as a means of getting early notice of learners likely to need special attention for one reason or another.

A *'warm up'* is a brief activity to do at the beginning of a lesson for any of the following reasons: to get your students' attention, to review and recycle previous learning, to help your students get in the mood to work with others, to cheer them up or wake them up if they seem tired or bored, to calm them down if they are over-excited, to introduce the theme of work to follow, to create a buffer period during which latecomers can be absorbed relatively easily, to make students want to come on time, to encourage a positive attitude towards English, and to help build a feeling of group solidarity.

A *'break'* is a brief change of pace or change of focus activity for the middle of a lesson in order to signal the boundary between two quite different units of work, to revive learners' concentration if it flags after a long period of doing the same sort of work, or to change the mood of a class for one reason or another. (For instance, a quiet, reflective break may be advisable between a lively discussion and a writing activity.)

A '*closer*' is a brief activity to do just before the end of a lesson, to review and summarise what has been covered earlier in the lesson, to send your students out of class in a good mood, to exercise skills or work on aspects of language that have been neglected in the lesson so far, to give your students something useful and interesting to do if they have finished your main activities sooner than you expected, and to provide a sense of closure.

To a certain extent, the ordering of the activities in this chapter reflects my hunches about when in a course or lesson teachers are most likely to do each one. For instance, ice-breakers come first while activities that seem best as closers come last.

2.1 Clap and say

Age	9 and up
Level	All
Time	5 minutes
Focus	Rhythm, concentration, learning names
Function	Ice-breaker, warm up, closer; the variations can serve as warm ups, breaks or closers

Procedure

1 Everyone stands in a circle.
2 Begin the activity as follows:
   a Everyone, all together, claps their hands twice.
   b All together, everyone holds their hands apart (palms up) as if offering something to the group.
   c The first person says their name into the space above their palms.
   d Everyone claps their hands twice.
   e The next person in the circle repeats Step (c).
   f Everyone repeats Step (d) and so on around the circle like this: *Clap, clap, (name), clap, clap, (name)* . . .
   g Finish with two claps.
3 Go around the circle again in the same way, but a bit faster and without breaking the rhythm.

Follow on
In a fairly small class, go right around the circle with each name, e.g. *Clap, clap, Maria, clap, clap,* . . .

Otherwise, ask everyone to learn the names of the person to their left and to their right. Then, once around the circle, everyone says the name of the person on their left, and again around the circle everyone says the name of the person on their right.

Variations

*   Instead of their name, students call out a hobby or passion of theirs, or a favourite colour or food.
*   Each student chooses an item of vocabulary from the previous lesson or from a text they have just read and says that instead of their own name.

Acknowledgement

I first experienced this activity in a workshop with British teachers of English in primary schools led by Diana Spratt.

Jean Rüdiger-Harper

2.2 Passing on

Age	13 and up
Level	Pre-intermediate–Advanced
Time	5–10 minutes
Focus	Imperatives, use of vocabulary related to clothing and parts of the body
Function	Warm up, closer

Procedure

1   Everyone stands in a circle or line. If you are all in a line, you should stand in the middle.
2   Pass an object such as a book or a pen to the person on your left and another object to the person on your right saying *Pass it on, please.*
3   When everyone has got the idea, explain that now people will 'pass on' commands that others have to carry out. As an example, start with something like *Touch your nose!* or *Touch your trousers!*, which students in turn first do and then repeat to a neighbour. Encourage students to be really quick.
4   Send a command left and another one to the right.
5   When a command gets back to you, stop it and pass on a new one.
6   Get everyone's attention. Say that now each of them should start a command chain in the same direction, all at the same time. Add that everyone should stop talking once their own command has returned to them.
7   Repeat Step 6, with commands going in the opposite direction.

Follow on
- Explain that the basic idea will now be to say something different from what you have touched. For instance, you touch your head but say *Foot*. Then the person next to you has to do the opposite very quickly such as touch their foot and say *Head*, then say a different 'opposite command' to their neighbour, who also does its opposite and then says a new opposite command to *their* neighbour and so on. Before starting this phase for real, stage a brief demonstration. Then begin.
- If your students are very good at this and seem to be enjoying it, ask them to start a new round at different points of the circle simultaneously. To make the activity more energetic, tell everyone to touch with their nose or an elbow rather than with their hands.

Variation
For a longer activity that can serve as a closer, make things more competitive either by getting students to drop out if they make a mistake (in word or action), or by collecting forfeits. In the latter case, students will need to do something (e.g. sing, tell a joke) to get back their place in the circle.

Acknowledgement
This is an adaptation of an old school game I found in a Hungarian collection of games (*Nagy játékkönyv*, Könyvkuckó, Budapest, 1996).

Judit Fehér

2.3 Flash the picture

Age	Any
Time	5 minutes
Level	Post-beginner–Advanced
Focus	Nouns and prepositions especially, but other elements of language too, depending on the picture
Material	A large picture on stiff paper or a copy on OHP transparency
Function	Warm up, lead-in

This activity is particularly useful for getting everyone's attention at the beginning of a lesson or at the beginning of a new unit of work after a lesson has begun. It is also a good way of exploiting a picture that relates to a theme or text you plan to use later in the lesson.

Preparation
See p. 8.

Procedure
See p. 8.

Variations
- Find two pictures which (1) show the same things but in different places or (2) show basically the same things but with a dozen or so minor differences (e.g. in one picture a woman has a scarf and in the other she does not). Display the picture (and keep it displayed). Flash the other one. Elicit differences.
- Write a description of a picture which differs in about a dozen details from the picture you are going to flash. Make a class set of the text, hand it out and give everyone time to read it. Flash your picture. Elicit differences between the text and the picture.
- For a longer, more competitive activity, form mixed-proficiency teams of four or five. In each team, choose as secretary one of the team's least proficient members. Tell everyone they will have to whisper within their teams so that competing teams will not be able to hear them. Flash the picture for just a few seconds. Secretaries write lists of people and objects seen. Call time. Collect the lists. Declare a winner. Hold up the picture and elicit comment about it. Repeat with two or three other pictures.

Acknowledgement
I learned the main activity at Pilgrims in 1985.

Seth Lindstromberg

2.4 Alphabetical vocabulary review

Age	Any
Level	Any
Time	5–10 minutes
Focus	Review of recently encountered vocabulary
Function	Warm up, break, closer

Procedure
1 Write the alphabet on the board in a circle, in a 'V' pattern or in some other shape (e.g. in a spiral or the shape of a fish). Circle *J*, *K*, *Q*, *X*, *Y*, *Z*.

2 Point to *A* and ask if anyone can remember a word or very short phrase beginning with that letter – for example, something they learned in the lesson before or (if you are doing this activity as a closer) the lesson you are about to finish.

3 As soon as someone calls out an appropriate word, cross out the letter *A* and point to *B*. Ask for a recently learned vocabulary item that begins with *that* letter. Move briskly through the alphabet in this way. At each letter, allow a maximum of about seven seconds. Whenever no one calls out anything suitable within this time, move on to the next letter. As you continue through the alphabet in this way, periodically point to a letter you have already crossed out and ask *What was that word again?* When you come to the circled letters, ask just for a word – recently learned or not – which contains the letter somewhere.

4 When you reach the end of the alphabet, go back to any letters not crossed out and give students a bit more time to call out a word for each.

5 On the board, write any of the vocabulary that you think some of the class perhaps did not hear or might have forgotten and clarify meaning and usage as necessary.

Variations

- Specify the vocabulary to be reviewed in different ways. For example, ask students to call out vocabulary from a recently read short story, or ask them only for words with two or more syllables.

- Choose a student who has not yet mastered the names of the letters of the alphabet and give him or her the job of calling out each letter as you point to it. Tell this student to give a hand signal if he or she wants any whispered help from students sitting nearby.

- For a longer review activity (about 15 minutes), ask students to work in pairs or threes. They arrange the alphabet any way they like and then use their notebooks to find the vocabulary that they need and include it on their sheets. Encourage them to be artistic (but remind them not to be too slow). As students finish their lists, they stick them up on the wall. As more and more lists go up, students mill around looking at what others have done. Encourage questions about meaning. Ask everyone to sit down. Ask which lists are the fullest and which are the most artistic.

- For the difficult letters, ask students to think of a word which includes (rather than begins with) these letters. Or ask students to do this for all letters. (A disadvantage of this latter procedure, however, is that the *beginnings* of words are more likely to be stored in memory than anything in the middle.)

Example arrangements

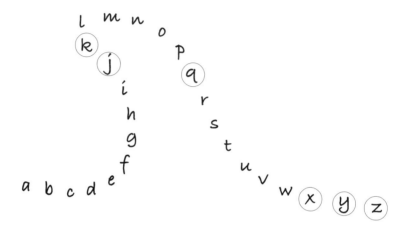

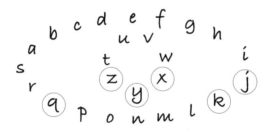

Comment
The device of arranging the alphabet in an unexpected shape helps get students' attention.

Seth Lindstromberg

2.5 Surprise questions

Age	11 and up
Level	Elementary–Advanced
Time	5–10 minutes
Focus	Dramatic intonation and rhythm, the grammar of two kinds of *Wh-* questions
Function	Warm up, closer, lead-in to activities involving the use of the relevant types of *Wh-* question

Procedure

1 On the board sketch two people, A and B, facing each other. A says *I saw Jill up in a tree*. B says *You saw **who** up in a tree?!*
2 Say that B is very surprised by A's sentence. Invite the class to guess why. Accept any suitable guess – e.g. *Jill is 90 years old*, *Jill is a baby*, *Jill is a dog*. If no one offers a suitable reason, give one yourself.
3 Say that people ask questions like B's especially when they have heard something but find it hard to believe and want confirmation and/or more information.
4 Model the pronunciation of the sentence, showing exaggerated disbelief.
5 Lead repetition practice. Encourage students to exaggerate the stress and pitch pattern.
6 Ask how – if B wasn't surprised – this surprise question would be changed into a normal question. The answer is *Who did you see?* Point out that the question word has been moved to the front of the question, which is where question words are in normal *Wh-* questions.

Follow on

• Introduce a new dialogue of the following form: A: *Ann ate a hamburger.* B: ***Who** ate a hamburger?!* Ask why B might be surprised – e.g. Ann is a vegetarian. Ask too how this second surprise question could be changed into a normal *Wh-* question. (The wording stays the same; only the intonation changes.) Give or elicit the rule about when we do and do not use a *do/does/did* in *Wh-* questions. Here is how it may be formulated in light of work on surprise questions:

'Think of the surprise question. Where is the *Wh-* word? In a normal *Wh-* question, the *Wh-* word is at the front. If it is not at the front in the surprise question, you have to move it there to make a normal *Wh-* question. And if you do move it, you put in a *do/does/did* (if there is no other auxiliary already). But if the *Wh-* word is already at the front in the surprise question, then the grammar of the normal and the surprise questions are exactly the same – there is no *do/does/did*.'

- Ask students to:
  - a write their own surprise question dialogues
  - b think of one or more reasons why Person B could be surprised
  - c rewrite their dialogue so that the question is a normal *Wh-* question

Comment

- This activity may lose much of its value as a warm up if you stress the grammar point more than pronunciation.
- The explanation given above is meant to complement, not supplant, more traditional ways of dealing with '*do* insertion' in *Wh-* questions.

Example dialogues

A: *Jack threw his TV out of his window.*
B: *Jack did **what**?!*

A: *Dracula has stopped drinking blood.*
B: ***Who** has stopped drinking blood?!*

A: *Margaret drinks 20 cups of coffee a day.*
B: *Margaret drinks **how many** cups a day?!*

A: *I failed my test because the moon was full.*
B: *You failed your test **why**?!*

A: *May went on holiday with Ann.*
B: ***Who** went on holiday with **who**?!*

(Note, 'double surprise' questions like this cannot be straightforwardly changed to normal *Wh-* questions.)

Seth Lindstromberg

2.6 From letters to grammar

Age	11 and up
Level	Elementary–Advanced
Time	5–10 minutes
Focus	Aural recognition of letters of the alphabet, the structure of phrases and clauses, oral accuracy, (variations) vocabulary review
Function	Warm up, closer

Procedure

1 Explain the rules, as follows:
   a You will call out letters in groups of four, e.g. *A, D, I, F*. Add that you will avoid infrequent letters such as *X*.
   b When you call out a set of four letters, everyone should try to think of a grammatical and meaningful four-word phrase or sentence that uses each letter as the first letter of a word. The order of the letters is not important, so *A dog in France* and *I found a dollar* are both acceptable.
   c After they have had time to write down an idea or two, you will call time and ask what they have written.

2 Start with an example of just three letters.

Variations

- Say that you are going to call out short 'initials' of phrases they have met sometime during the previous week, or in a particular song they have heard or in a story they have recently read. Say that you will award points for *any* grammatical combination of words but give an extra point if they have been able to 'read your mind' and say the precise phrase you were thinking of.

- Form groups of four or so. Everyone prepares a few initials of recently learned phrases. They all take turns being 'teacher' (as in the first Variation).

Seth Lindstromberg

2.7 Comparing it and me

Age	11 and up
Level	Elementary–Advanced
Time	10 minutes
Focus	Comparing, contrasting, (optional) poetic metaphor
Function	Warm up

Because this warm up encourages students to think outside of normal classifications, it is a particularly good lead-in to many longer creative thinking activities.

Preparation

Bring an object to class – a soccer ball, for example, or a potato.

Procedure

1   Ask if anybody can say one way in which your object is different from them, e.g. *It is small but I am big.* When you get one statement, try to elicit several more.

2   Ask everyone to think of from one to five ways in which they and the ball are *similar*, e.g. *I am in this room. The ball is also here,* and write these ideas down in sentence form. Say you will give them a minute or so to think. Add that they can use bilingual dictionaries.

3   Ask them what they have written.

Follow on

- As a warm up in later lessons ask your students to call out five things they have in common with the object of the day.
- Do this activity before you present a song or poem that draws analogies between two quite different things.

Comment

- I have used this activity with a wide variety of objects including an apple, a glass of water, a chocolate bar wrapper, a small bell and a rolled up section of a newspaper.
- If you want ideas to come freely, avoid encouraging students to use any particular forms of comparison or contrast.

Seth Lindstromberg

2.8   Kill the text (then bring it back to life)

Age	11 and up
Level	Elementary–Advanced
Time	10 minutes; 15 minutes with the optional Step 5
Focus	Accuracy in speech and (optionally) writing; listening to others
Function	Closer; Variation 3 is a pre-reading/pre-listening activity

Procedure

See p. 3.

Variations

- Students who volunteer are likely to be among the most proficient. In order to give your least proficient students a chance to speak, begin to call on students by name after one volunteer has said a sentence and thus enabled you to clearly demonstrate how the activity works. Call mainly on your less proficient learners but each time you erase one of their words, ask *Did anyone else have a sentence for that word?* This gives the more proficient students a chance to participate.

- Between Steps 2 and 3, allow time for students to write a sentence using one of their words.
- Use this activity to preview the content of a listening or a longer reading text. For example, use a short extract from a short story. After Step 5, elicit guesses and other comments about the likely character and plot of the work as a whole.

Tips (Steps 3–4)

- Bits of cheerful banter help the activity along. For example, STUDENT: *Fruit. I like fruit.* TEACHER: *Which kind especially?*
- Just to keep everyone on their toes, occasionally ask particular students to repeat a sentence that another student has just said or even a sentence that another student said some time before.
- If it turns out that there are some words that no one has chosen, ask who can spontaneously think up statements for them.
- It is particularly important to do Steps 1–4 briskly. Quickly move to another student if anyone is struggling to think of something to say.

Acknowledgement

The core idea for this activity comes from Randal Holme.

Seth Lindstromberg

2.9 Question–question improvisation dialogues

Age	13 and up
Level	Intermediate–Advanced
Time	10 minutes
Focus	Question formation, spontaneity, listening intently to a partner, replying relevantly according to rules
Function	Warm up, closer

Procedure

1 Divide the class into pairs and say that in a minute they will be having conversations totally composed of questions.
2 Give an example conversation. For example:

A: *How are you?*→B: *What did you say?*→A: *How are you?*→B: *Why do you ask? Do I look ill?*→A: *Don't you feel ill?*→B: *Are you a doctor?*

3   Teach the class a repertoire of questions that can be especially useful:

What did you say?   Can you say that again?   Are you deaf?
Am I mad?   Can we stop this?   Why do you ask?

4   Explain that if someone answers without using a question, they lose a point.
5   The conversations begin.

Variation
Students work in threes. Two conduct a dialogue and one keeps score and keeps track of time. They change roles at regular intervals.

Acknowledgement
I got this idea from the UK Channel 4 TV comedy-cum-improvisation show *Whose line is it anyway?*

Tessa Woodward

2.10 Alphabet improvisation dialogues

Age	13 and up
Level	Pre-intermediate–Advanced
Time	10 minutes
Focus	Spontaneity, listening intently to a partner, replying relevantly while following strict rules
Function	Warm up, closer

Procedure
1   On the board, write the alphabet but leave out *k*, *q*, *x* and *z*.
2   Tell the class that in a minute, in pairs, they will be having 'alphabet' dialogues like this one:

A: *Can I borrow some money?*
B: *Do you think I am rich or something?*
A: *Even a little would help.*
B: *Fifty pence?*
A: *Good. Thank you.*
B: *How do I know you will pay me back?*
A: *I will. Don't worry. Please hurry. I need it now.*
B: *Just a minute.* etc.

That is, if A says something beginning with *c*, B's response must begin with the next letter of the alphabet, which is *d*; and A's response to that must begin with the next letter after *d*, which is *e*, and so on until they get through the alphabet (although they skip *k*, *q*, *x* and *z*).

3 Tell the students to pair up and begin.

4 End the activity when a few pairs have gone through the whole alphabet once.

Follow on
Students write alphabet dialogues for homework.

Tip
Step 3: Pairs may find it easier to get started if you say that the letter which Student A starts with should be the first letter of Student B's name. Or else write a few words on the board and say that the As can begin their dialogues with any one of those words, e.g. *Hello, If, Don't, Let's, Why*.

Variations
- Make the activity easier by saying that the letter that must be used can come at the beginning of *any* word: A: <u>A</u>re you ready? B: I'm sorry, <u>b</u>ut ready for what? A: <u>C</u>an't you stop joking? Our wedding is today. B: I <u>d</u>on't think you told me about it.
- If you choose the easy option, put students in threes. Two students do the dialogue and one counts points: two points if the letter is used at the very beginning of the first word, one point if it is used somewhere else, minus one point if the alphabet rule is broken.
- Pairs play against pairs. Students A and B take one role and Students C and D take the other. When it is the turn of A and B, for example, either one can speak, depending on who has an idea first. (This usually speeds up the activity quite a bit.)
- Students go through the alphabet backwards or, instead of going through the alphabet, students go through the letters of a word or phrase. For example, if the phrase is *Famous people*, Student A says something beginning with *f*. B's reply must begin with *a*, A's reply to that must begin with *m*, and so on.

Acknowledgement
This is a slight adaptation of an activity sometimes played on the UK Channel 4 TV improvisation show *Whose line is it anyway?*

Tessa Woodward

Other short activities usable as warm ups (W), breaks (B) or closers (C)

- Fluency: 3.4 (W/C), 3.5 (C), 3.6 (W), 3.11 (W/C), 3.12 (W/C), 9.1 (W/C), 9.3 (W/C), 9.4 (W/C, but not the 1st time you do the activity)
- Listening: 4.3 (W/C)
- Vocabulary: 7.2 (W/C), 7.3 (W/C), 7.9 (W/B/C), 7.10 (W/B/C), 7.11 (C) (Note: 7.10 needs to have been set up in an earlier lesson.)
- Literature: 8.3 (C), 8.5 (W/C), 8.7 (W/B/C)

3 Mainly speaking

A major purpose of this chapter is to provide procedures that can make young adolescents *want* to speak English.

Each of the activities can serve one or more of the following four roles:

- a topically relevant lead-in to, or follow on from, other work that you plan to do
- the major component of a lesson
- a short ongoing component of several, or many, lessons (e.g. 3.11 'Letter on the board' and 3.12 '30-second stimulus talks') which can, on occasion, play the role of a warm up or break
- a closer (i.e. a short activity to do just before the end of a lesson)

Oral fluency in pairs and groups: instructing, conversing, interviewing

3.1 LEGO® constructions

Age	11 and up
Level	Low-intermediate–Advanced
Time	15–20 minutes
Focus	General oral fluency, communicative accuracy in giving and comprehending oral instructions, (follow on) writing and reading instructions
Material	LEGO® building bricks, (optional) paper towels

This is a classic 'information gap' activity in which the effectiveness of students' instructions can be checked against a tangible model.

Preparation
1 Get enough LEGO® bricks for the students to have at least ten each.
2 Plan how to pre-teach/revise the language needed to describe the different bricks. (One option is to elicit an invented name for each of the different types of brick.)
3 Plan how to pre-teach/revise the language of giving instructions (e.g. *First you must/should put the long brick on your desk. Next take the square white brick and . . .*).

Procedure

1 Do any necessary pre-teaching.
2 Put the students in pairs of pairs that face each other across a desk, and ask them all to make a book barrier between themselves and the pair opposite, like this:

S | S
S | S
↑ ↑
Pair A Pair B

3 Each pair working together gets an identical set of LEGO® bricks which they use to make a structure which the pair opposite them *must not see.*
4 Pair A (but not Pair B) break up their structure, but leave their bricks on the desk.
5 Pair B explain how to make their structure and Pair A use their bricks to try to reconstruct it *without looking across the book barrier.*
6 When Pair B have finished their instructions, the pairs compare structures.
7 Pair A remakes its model, and Pair B breaks up its model and the process is repeated.

Follow on

The students write down the instructions for making their structure. They leave these instructions on their desk and move to another desk and, following the instructions left there by another pair, try to build the corresponding structure.

Variations

• Use Cuisenaire rods instead of LEGO® bricks.
• Students describe to each other:
  – maps and floor plans
  – routes on a map
  – sketches and pictures (see 4.3 'Picture dictation').

Tip

Hand out paper towels or similar and ask students to lay them over their finished structures in order to hide them better. When they describe their structures, they can peek under their (own) towels as necessary.

Comment

By putting pairs with pairs as above (i.e. one pair on one side of a table and another pair on the other) you:

- halve the number of LEGO® bricks you need
- approximately halve the noise produced
- create various options for forming pairs, e.g. pairing good speakers with ones who are weaker
- tend to increase the likelihood that listeners will get the information they need

Acknowledgement
I first encountered this kind of activity in Byrne and Rixon (1979).

David A. Hill

3.2 Describe and draw . . . the opposite

Age	12 and up
Level	Elementary–Advanced
Time	15 minutes
Focus	General oral fluency, communicative accuracy in giving and comprehending oral instructions
Material	At least half a class set of suitable pictures

This is an information gap activity with an unusual twist. It is fun to do after doing more conventional 'describe and draw' exercises – see 4.3 'Picture dictation' and the final variation of 3.1.

Procedure
1 Students pair up and decide who is Student A and who is B.
2 Explain that:
   a Each A will get a picture to describe to B. But Student B should draw something *opposite* to what A says. For example, if A says *There is a man* B should draw a child, a woman, a dog, a ghost – anything that B thinks is the opposite of a man. If A says there is a tree in the foreground, B may draw a telephone pole in the background.
   b They will then compare pictures.
   c B will then try to tell A what A's actual instructions were.
3 As and Bs swap roles. Give B a picture and collect A's picture and give it to a B in another pair (unless you have enough pictures to give each student one of their own).
4 Organise a mini-exhibition of what your students have drawn.

Variations

- Step 2c: At lower-intermediate level and above, B also explains to A – in cases of doubt – just how it is that a figure in his/her drawing is the opposite of what A said, e.g. *A telephone pole is the opposite of a tree because, if it is made of wood, it is a dead tree, which is the opposite of a living tree.*
- Each pair gets only one picture. When A has described the picture, B either uses the same picture or his/her own 'oppositised' drawing of it.

Hanna Kryszewska

3.3 The same but different

Age	12 and up
Level	Pre-intermediate–Advanced
Time	15 minutes
Focus	Conversing about pictures, topic-related vocabulary, expressions of comparison, (second variation) writing
Material	Colour photos/reproductions of houses, holy day scenes or streets – one identical or similar photo per pair

Preparation

Each pair needs a colour picture of a street, a house or a scene relating to an important holy day (e.g. Christmas, Diwali), traditional festival or holiday, or similar. The pictures that all the pairs look at need not be identical but the subject should be the same for everyone. (Check your coursebook for suitable pictures.)

Procedure

1 Ask everyone to pair up. Then give out the pictures or name the book and page where a suitable picture may be found.
2 Tell the pairs to use their picture to talk about their own world and experience as follows. If, for example, they have a picture of a street, they each talk about their *own* street: how it is similar to and different from the one in the picture, what the picture reminds them of and so on.
3 When conversations begin to taper off, tell everyone they are going to form new pairs so that each student can tell someone else what their first partner said. Say that now is the time (before they actually form new pairs) to make sure they remember what their first partner said.
4 Students move into their new pairs and converse as just instructed.

Follow on

With the whole class, lead a discussion around the issue of what their streets (or whatever) have in common.

Variations

- After Step 2, pairs split up. Students get sheets of paper and draw what their partner has told them. For example, they draw the partner's street, complete with labels. Before moving on to their new partner, everyone asks their first partner to check whether the drawing of his or her street is accurate.
- After Step 2, students each write down what their partner told them and then ask this partner to check the writing for factual accuracy. Pairs then swap each other's texts and read them.

Hanna Kryszewska

3.4 Newspaper pictures

Age	11 and up
Level	Pre-intermediate–Advanced
Time	5–20 minutes
Focus	Conversing about pictures, expressing likes/dislikes, comparing and contrasting, general fluency
Material	A class set of pictures from newspapers or magazines

In this activity students each speak to a partner about a picture. It is the instructions which you call out at intervals that make this an especially dependable way of generating conversation which is on task.

Preparation

1 Cut out enough pictures from old newspapers or magazines for each learner to have one. Aim for a mix of news pictures and adverts.
2 Pre-sort the pictures so that, when you hand them out, adjacent students have ones that are quite different.

Procedure

1 Distribute the pictures and ask the students to look at them in silence for a few moments.
2 Say that shortly you will be giving them some topic instructions concerning their pictures. Add that each time you specify a topic, everyone should say something about it to their partner and that they

should each begin by speaking about their own picture. Each time you announce a topic, let the exchanges run out before announcing the next one.

a Say something factual about your picture, e.g. *This is a picture of a big red American car.*

b Say something you like and/or do not like about it and why, e.g. *I like the house just next to the beach, because it looks old and interesting.*

c Say something it reminds you of, e.g. *This restaurant is like the one I went to on holiday in Spain last year.*

d Talk about something in your picture which is related to something in your partner's, e.g. *The apples in my picture were grown in the garden in yours.*

e Each of you say one way in which the two pictures are different, e.g. *My picture was taken in the city and yours in the country.*

f Say something about what is on the back, e.g. *There is part of an article about politics in Australia, and part of an advert for some kind of new mobile phone.*

Follow on

- In pairs, they write a paragraph which links the two original pictures in detail (e.g. as part of a mini-story or a description).
- (1) Everyone gets up and finds a partner / some partners who has/have a similar picture. (2) Ask pairs/groups to tell the rest of the class why they are together (e.g. *We're together because we both/all have pictures which show places with water in them*). (3) Anyone who is on their own gives a reason why they have no partners, and the rest of the class can suggest who else they can join.

Variation

Step 2: If you want the activity to be short and snappy, ask your students to limit what they say to just one sentence.

Tips

- It is a good idea to use either all colour or all black and white pictures and not mix cartoons or drawings with photographs.
- At Step 1, suggest that everyone should conceal their picture from their partner until you say they can show it. Step 2b is a good point for this to happen.

Summary of cues

Say something factual about your picture.

Say something you like and/or do not like about it and why.

Say something it reminds you of.

Talk about something in your picture which is related to something in your partner's.

Each of you say one way in which the two pictures are different.

Say something about what is on the back.

David A. Hill

3.5 My map of the world

Age	12 and above
Level	Pre-intermediate–Advanced
Time	15–30 minutes
Focus	Conversing, vocabulary (e.g. names of countries, abstract nouns)
Material	A map showing a very simple outline of the world

Preparation

1 Make A4 or A3 photocopies of a world map, one per student. (The Internet is a good source of originals.)

2 Make a list of 10–15 nouns to use in the dictation (see p. 64). Suitable concrete nouns are ones that refer to interesting:
   - things and materials that can be present in or produced in a country
   - activities that can happen in a country

   Suitable nouns may vary greatly in type and may refer, for instance, to:
   - states of affairs (e.g. *conflict*)
   - emotions (e.g. *love*)
   - states of mind (e.g. *spirituality*)

   If possible, include two or three words that are likely to be new to your class.

Example nouns

Nouns that are (relatively) concrete:

Pre-intermediate: *oil, good cars, good food, lots of fresh water, good chocolate, sand, tea, good coffee, elephants, money, good music, dancing, good films, bad films, great art*

Intermediate: The above, plus *high fashion, spicy food, good surfing, high technology, mountain climbing, night life, earthquakes*

Advanced: The above, plus *precious metals, gemstones, hydro-electric power, a booming economy, an ailing economy*

Nouns that are (relatively) abstract:

Elementary: *fun, happiness, good government, danger, peace, magic, stress, progress*

Intermediate: The above, plus *mystery, adventure, knowledge, prosperity, democracy, corruption, tolerance, conflict, excitement, mystery, famine*

Advanced: The above, plus *spirituality, strife, traditions of literacy, oppression, diversity, inventiveness, rule of law, a wide income gap, stereotyped gender roles, superstition, practicality, dogmatism, low/high material standard of living*

Procedure

1   Give out maps to students and tell them that you will dictate words and they should write these words on their maps where they think they belong. For example, if you say *Coffee*, they can write the word on Italy (because Italian coffee is good) or Brazil (because it is a coffee-growing country). That is, they can write the word anywhere provided they can justify their decision. But only one location per word!

2   Dictate your words. (Start with four or five concrete nouns and then switch to ones that are abstract. *Happiness* and *love* are good ones to finish with at all levels.)

3   In pairs or threes, students compare and discuss their placement of the words.

Variations

• Write the words on the board one by one.

• Dictate adjectives. Elementary: *hot, cold, wet, snowy, friendly, exciting, dangerous, crowded*; Intermediate: *under-populated, troubled, technologically advanced, picturesque*; Advanced: *volatile, geographically varied, a ticking time bomb, hidebound.*

- For low-level monolingual groups reluctant to use English when speaking to each other, after dictating the words ask students, *silently*, to write sentences of the form, *I put .... in .... because ....* Then they show each other their maps and read each other their sentences. Or, assign the writing as homework. Students tell each other what they wrote after you have corrected and handed back their work.
- Rather than write words on maps, students write them on a blank sheet of paper along with the name of one country, e.g. *coffee–Brazil*. But this is somewhat more difficult than the main procedure, since having a map seems to motivate students and, as well, is a source of information about spelling and, of course, what countries are where.

Acknowledgements
This activity was inspired by the out of the ordinary dictation activities in Davis and Rinvolucri (1988).

Hanna Kryszewska

3.6 Be someone else

Age	11 and up
Level	Post-beginner–Advanced
Time	5–15 minutes
Focus	Listening to information, asking questions, oral fluency, (follow on) writing about an invented character
Material	(Optional) props, e.g. a hat

This activity begins with you entering the classroom in the role of an imaginary character, in order to prepare students for the task of performing characters of their own invention.

Preparation
The object of this exercise is to bring somebody new into the classroom. To that end, you should prepare to act as someone very different from yourself, and from people your learners have encountered in the coursebook. Write out and learn by heart a biography for your new self, and you may wish to use props: clothes, accessories such as a hat or pipe or other objects that might help indicate someone's character or occupation.

Procedure
1 Enter the class in role. Tell them that their normal teacher cannot come for a while because he or she is busy and that you have been asked to fill

in the lesson. Give them some basic pieces of information about your new self.

2   Get the students to ask questions about you. If necessary, prompt (*Elias, ask me about . . .*).

3   When they have found out all you had planned about your new self, leave the classroom and come back in as your teacher self.

4   Ask the class who looked after them before you arrived, and elicit a few pieces of information from the whole class.

5   Ask the students to work in pairs and write notes about what they can remember about the person.

6   When they have finished, elicit information from the pairs, and try to build the whole picture from the whole class.

Follow on

- Tell the students that, as pairs, they are going to invent two characters who are connected in some way. Suggest they try to make them as unusual as possible. Circulate and help them with vocabulary.
- When they are ready, each pair should perform their characters to another pair who should ask questions in order to learn more about the characters being performed.
- Students write about their newly invented character pairing.

Variation

Instead of taking on a whole new personality, tell the students only one interesting thing about yourself which they have to use as the cue for their questions. Some possibilities: *I have a pet elephant at home, I've just come back from a year alone on a desert island, I have twenty children, I took part in a Hollywood movie last year, I met the President of the United States, Sometimes I become invisible, My friends gave me a surprise party last week.* They think of any possible questions which a reporter might ask, and you improvise answers. This works best if you take the situation totally seriously, trying to sound as convincing as possible.

Comment

- The first teacher I saw taking on a role like this was a DTEFLA candidate in Munich in 1988. The student–student follow up is my development of the idea. Mario Rinvolucri writes about something similar in Rinvolucri (1993).
- The variation comes from Penny Ur.

David A. Hill

3.7 Picture interviews

Age	14 and up
Level	Pre-intermediate–Advanced
Time	25–40 minutes
Focus	Interview-like dialogue, the usefulness of follow on questions, adopting someone else's point of view
Material	Pictures from the print media, (optional) class set of a handout (pp. 69–70)

Preparation

Collect and photocopy unstaged, unposed pictures from newspapers and magazines that show non-celebrities in interesting settings, especially out of doors. It is best to provide enough pictures so that each student can choose from among three or more.

Procedure

1 Explain what the difference is between a 'primary' and a 'follow on' question and give a couple of examples (see pp. 69–70).

2 Form pairs and distribute your pictures. Say that everybody should look at all the pictures that are available but choose only one, which must be different from the one chosen by their partner.

3 Tell everyone to choose *one* person in their picture and indicate their choice by drawing an arrow or making a dot (in a bright colour, if possible) directly on the image of the person selected.

4 Say that everyone will enter the world shown in their picture, become the person they have marked, and be interviewed by their partner. Add that Student A should finish interviewing B before they swap roles (in Step 6).

5 Give everyone a copy of the handout showing the primary and follow on questions (pp. 69–70), remind everyone of the importance of asking questions of *both* kinds and start the first round of interviews.

6 Partners swap roles.

7 Bring the class together and ask different students to repeat something particularly memorable that their interviewee said.

Variation

• Do the A→B interviews in one lesson and the B→A interviews in another.

• If a number of your students are very weak relative to their partner, only do A→B interviews. That is, give the weakest students the reporters' handouts. The stronger students play the more difficult role of answering the questions.

- In groups of three, students speak as either a trainee reporter, local person, or trainee's boss so that each student has each role once, as follows. When in the role of 'boss', a student both listens to a trainee interview a local person and counts the number of follow on questions. After the interviews, bosses tell trainees how many follow on questions they asked and then ask trainees whether they think they have earned the right to keep their jobs.

Tips

- Just after Step 1: Mention that teachers find follow on questions particularly useful. Ask why. (Often people have more information to give than they include in a first answer.) Ask about other occupations in which follow on questions are useful and, again, ask why. (Police officers, lawyers, company personnel officers, psychologists and reporters are among those who make frequent use of follow on questions.)
- Step 5: Add that each Student A is going to interview their partner (B) in accordance with the following roles and (imagined) features of the situation:
  a The interviewee (B) is a person who lives in the area shown in the picture.
  b The interviewer (A) is a trainee reporter and this is his/her first major interview.
  c There is a cameraman (imaginary) on hand so of course each interview is going to be videoed for later transmission on TV.
  d The reporters' bosses will see the videos of the interviews. If a reporter (A) has done well – that is, asked enough follow on questions – he/she will get the job permanently and continue to be able to travel around the world and have adventures. But if their interview finishes too quickly, the reporter will lose the job and will have to go back to serving hamburgers (or whatever).
  e In each pair, the local person (B) shows their picture to A who interviews him/her using the handout.
- Step 5: Tell students that the exact questions they ask may vary, depending on their partner's picture.

Comment

The purpose of the list of questions is to encourage full participation by:

- students who ordinarily say little when in pairs
- students who all speak the same language and who are inclined to revert to their mother tongue

Even with relatively proficient and/or forthcoming students a fixed list of questions may be useful *the first time* you do an activity such as this in order to give them an idea of the range of questions that can be asked.

Handout for reporters (Pre-intermediate)

Primary questions

a   Tell us a few things about your life.
b   Do you have any routines in your everyday life?
c   What do you like best?
d   Who do you see and talk to most?
e   How do you feel about them/her/him?
f   Could you tell us a bit about your past?
g   Are things getting better or worse for you?
h   What is the hardest thing for you?
i   What do you think the future will bring?
j   Is there anything else you would like to say?

Follow on questions

Yes?   For example?
Why is that?   Could you tell me/us a bit more about . . . ?, etc.

Handout for reporters (Intermediate +)

Primary questions

a I wonder if you could tell us a few things about your life.

b Do you have any routines, any regular patterns, in your day-to-day life?

c Is there anything that especially cheers you up?

d Who do you have the most contact with?

e How do you feel about them/her/him?

f What is the exact nature of this/these relationship(s)?

g Could you tell us a bit about your past?

h Do you see any trends in your life? I mean, how are things getting better or worse for you?

i What is the hardest thing for you?

j So, in a nutshell, what kind of life do you have?

k What do you think the future has in store for you?

l Is there anything else you would like to say?

Follow on questions

Yes?   And?   And so?   For example?

And that is because . . . ?   Why is that?

Could you tell us/me why?

Could you tell me/us a bit more about . . . ?, etc.

Seth Lindstromberg

3.8 Tell me about it

Age	11 and up
Level	Pre-intermediate–Advanced
Time	25–35 minutes
Focus	Conversation, (follow on) narrative writing

Preparation

Think of something memorable that you did just one time or which happened to you just once and sum it up in the shortest possible sentence.

For instance, a friend of mine and I were fishing in a canoe once and the canoe capsized. A good sentence for this event is: *It turned over.*

Procedure

1 Write your sentence on the board and explain any possibly unfamiliar vocabulary.
2 Dictate several appropriate questions, such as, *What was 'it'?*, *When did this happen?* and then invite students to ask them to you, along with additional questions too. In each of your answers, give a bit more information than the question actually requires.
3 When your class has heard more or less the full story behind your sentence, ask them each to write a similarly brief sentence about something they did or which happened to them – something positive (e.g. *I won*) or not (e.g. *I fell off*). Stress that their (true) sentence:
   - should be about something that happened only once
   - should *not* give information about when, where, who with or anything else beyond the minimum, e.g. not *Our boat turned over.*
4 When everyone has a sentence, put students in groups of three. Add that one student in each group should show his/her sentence and answer questions until the full story is out. The other two students each do the same, in turn.

Follow on

Students write a partner's story out in full. If this is done in class, they can periodically check the facts with the person they are writing about.

Variations

- If most groups have finished but one or two students have not had an opportunity to answer questions about their sentences, note down these sentences and in a later lesson these students, in turn, take questions from the whole class.
- Students each sketch a place that they have visited one or more times – a place such as the house of grandparents, a campsite, a beach resort. In pairs or threes students show their sketches and answer questions. (This works particularly well in multi-national classes.)

Tips

- Step 2: If you are still feeling your way with your class, make this as brief as possible.
- Step 3: Some students will write a sentence very quickly while others will

ponder for a while. Ask early finishers to make a quick sketch to go with their sentence. If anyone simply cannot think of a sentence, put them with a threesome to make a group of four. ('No sentence' students virtually always think of one when they see how other students are doing the activity.)

Acknowledgement
The germ of this idea comes from a multi-stage writing activity by Christine Frank.

Seth Lindstromberg

3.9 Stories from pictures

Age	11 and up
Level	Pre-intermediate–Advanced
Time	20–30 minutes
Focus	Telling, listening to and retelling stories, (follow on) narrative writing
Material	Pictures, as described

In this activity students tell each other picture-based stories. In the end, everyone hears their original story told back to them and comments on how it has been changed.

Preparation
1 You need enough of the following types of pictures for pairs of students to have sets that include: a place in the town, a place in the country, a male, a female and an object. The pictures can be colour and black and white, mixed. They do not need to be stuck onto card or paper, but it is less distracting if they are. It is best if all the pictures are different.
2 Think how to form your class into pairs of pairs that work together like this: AA+BB and CC+DD, then AA+CC and BB+DD, then AA+DD and BB+CC.

Procedure
1 Put the class into pairs, and give each pair a picture of a place in the country, a place in the town, a male, a female and an object. If there is some incongruity between the pictures, it makes the activity more interesting.
2 Each pair makes up a story relating to the five pictures, including names of people and places.

3 When they are ready, put pairs in pairs so Pairs AA and BB (and CC and DD, etc.) tell each other their stories, using their pictures. Stress that:
   • they should listen very carefully to what they are told because they are going to have to retell each other's stories
   • when the stories are finished, they should swap pictures
4 Pairs move around so that AA tell BBs' story to CC, and CC tell DDs' story to AA, using the pictures they got from their previous partners. (At the same time, BB and DD tell each other their earlier partners' story.)
5 Pairs move again. DD and AA now sit together (while CC sit with BB). DD tell AAs' story back to AA who give them feedback about differences. At the same time, BB hear their own story back from CC.
6 The groups stay together and CC and DD hear their stories back.

Follow on
Individually or in pairs, students write their stories in more detail, possibly sticking the pictures next to the text. Students then exchange stories and read them. In a small class, if they all read each other's work, you can then have a discussion about which is the best story and why.

Variations
• Students work individually rather than in pairs. For this, though, you need more pictures.
• Vary the composition of the five picture sets, e.g.
  – Rather than having one picture of a place in the town and another in the country, include two pictures of places that are simply different (e.g. one in the city and one by the sea or one house that looks expensive and one that does not).
  – Have pictures of either places or means of transportation (e.g. a house and a ship, or a ship and a car).
  – Instead of a picture of a female and one of a male, have pictures of two females, or two males.

David A. Hill

3.10 Graffiti

Age	14–16
Level	Intermediate–Advanced
Time	30 minutes
Focus	Expressing opinions, writing short statements of opinion, discussing
Material	Large sheets of paper, broad-tip felt pens

In this activity students write short, graffiti-like texts on posters and discuss them in groups. It works particularly well if you know your students' mother tongue(s).

Preparation

1   Get several large sheets of paper: flip-chart size is best, but two or three sheets of A3 stuck together will work too. For a class of 40, eight large sheets may be sufficient.
2   At the top of each of the sheets write one of the following words: *Television, Computers, Cigarettes, Mobile phones, Money, Cars, Football, Love.* If you want to be more controversial with an older group you know can handle the topics well, you might substitute in ones such as: *Religion, Drugs, Alcohol, Politics.* Optionally, include topics of local and/or current interest.
3   Put the sheets up around the walls of the classroom, at writing height, or lie them flat on separate desks.

Procedure

1   Introduce the topic of graffiti by asking your students what the purpose of graffiti is (e.g. to protest about something you do not like), where you see it (walls, usually) and if they can tell you some examples they have seen recently that have to do with more or less political protest. (This will probably be in the mother tongue.)
2   Ask them to look at the topics on the large sheets and then to go and stand next to the topic they are most interested in.
3   Ask those standing near each poster to tell each other what it is about that topic (TV, or whatever) that they really like. Explain that they should give fairly full reasons such as, *I really enjoy watching TV because you can learn so much about people in other countries.*
4   Ask the students in the 'poster groups' to talk about what other people do not like about their topic, e.g. *Some people think TV is a waste of time because most of the programmes are soaps and quizzes.*
5   Ask them to turn these negative comments into graffiti and write them on their sheet, e.g. *TV soaps are a waste of time. TV quizzes are useless.*
6   Ask the students to go to the sheets for topics which they are *not* interested in, or do not like. They should read the graffiti that have been written, and write new graffiti of their own, different from the ones already there.

7 Students each return to their original topic sheet, and read and discuss what is there with others who have chosen the same sheet.

8 Deal with any language errors on the posters.

Follow on
Choose one or two of the topics (perhaps the ones which have been written about most) and discuss the comments with the whole class. I often find this a productive way of starting an informal debate.

Tip
Step 5: Ask them to write short, provocative statements rather than non-sentence graffiti such as *Rubbish!*

David A. Hill

Holding forth, being in the spotlight

3.11 Letter on the board

Age	11 and up
Level	Elementary–Advanced
Time	5 minutes or less
Focus	Spontaneity, fluency, holding the floor, sticking to a topic

This short fluency-in-pairs speaking activity gets students speaking ad lib on a small set of topics. It requires no preparation and so readily serves as a warm up, break or closer.

Procedure
1 Ask a student to pick a letter between *A* and *Z* (but not *X*). If the student says *S* (or whatever), write a large *S* on the board.

2 Ask the students to give you three nouns that start with *S*. They might, for example, say *sports, skateboard, summer*. Write these nouns on the board.

3 Pair the students up (one or more threesomes is OK) and ask them to decide who is A and who is B.

4 Tell them that in a minute each A has to choose one of the topics on the board – *summer*, for instance – and talk about it to their partner for 30 seconds. Tell them they should not worry about grammatical accuracy. They should say anything that comes into their heads even if it is just odd words and phrases. If A gets stuck, B can prompt with questions or suggestions.

5 Call *Start*. Stay at the front and time 30 seconds. Then call *Stop*.

6 Say that B has to choose a different topic and follow the same rules.

7 Call *Start*, time 30 seconds and call *Stop*.

8 (Optional) If you have any trios, do the activity one more time to make sure that all the students have had at least one chance to speak.

Follow on

- Once students have got used to speaking for 30 seconds (or whatever time you start with), make the time limit a bit longer.
- Students take turns speaking to a large group or to the whole class.

Tessa Woodward

3.12 30-second stimulus talks

Age	11 and up
Level	Lower-intermediate–Advanced
Time	Less than 5 minutes
Focus	Holding the floor, speaking in longer and longer turns, speaking to a group, encouraging students to take an interest in each other
Material	(In later lessons) Things brought in by students

Preparation

Decide what thing of yours you are going to talk about in Step 4.

Procedure *(as in a low-intermediate class)*

Setting the activity up

1 Explain that everyone will be giving one or more very short talks about an object.

2 Offer them a few opening and closing phrases such as:

   I'm going to talk about .... or I've decided to talk about .... or I've brought with me .... and That's it or That's all I want to say.

3 Teach some easy audience questions such as:
   Can you tell me more about ....?

4 Give a very short talk yourself, one of no more than 30 seconds, and speak very slowly. For example:
   I've decided to talk to you about my bicycle bell. I've brought it in so you can see it. It's very old. I like the sound it makes. I never clean it. That's it.

The prime aim here is not to give a really interesting talk about your object but rather to show your students that talking about an object is easy.

5　Ask students to bring in photos, objects, talismans, mascot toys and so on.

Student presentations

6　In later lessons, invite one or more students who have brought something in to sit at the front and 'show and tell' in English.

Follow on
- Once students have got used to speaking for 30 seconds (or whatever time you start with), make the time limit a bit longer.
- Try to elicit more and more audience questions.

Tips
- Call students up to present when there is a good, relaxed atmosphere in class.
- If a student is still talking fluently after 30 seconds have gone by, allow them to continue. But if they do go over, as soon as they start hesitating, gently bring them to a halt by congratulating them for speaking longer than the specified time. The point of initially specifying a 30-second time limit is to make students approach the task thinking it will be relatively easy to do.

Tessa Woodward

3.13　Pitching a wonderful new product

Age	12 and up
Level	Intermediate–Advanced
Time	25–40 minutes
Focus	Addressing a group, phrases and sentences for structuring spoken discourse and managing formal discussions
Material	A poster or a class set of handouts of a 'discourse skeleton', a sheet of paper for each student

Preparation

1　Make a list of non-complex things people use in everyday life, e.g. *pencil, chopsticks, fork, paper clip, sock, hat, shoe, coat hanger, umbrella, safety pin, glove* or *mitten, candle, needle, nail file*. You need enough so that

each student in a group of six or so students will have a different object (but students in *different groups* can have the same object).
2 Prepare a talk skeleton such as the one on p. 80.
3 Write *APPLAUSE!* (in huge letters) on a sheet of paper. (See the example presentation on p. 81 for its use.)

Procedure
1 Say a word or two about how important it can be for an inventor to be able to persuade potential investors, or a bank manager, that his or her invention is truly wonderful. *Many a fine invention has been lost to us because an inventor was unable to persuade investors . . .* That kind of thing. Say something too about the importance of having a prototype (i.e. a first example of an invention) for investors to look at.
2 Display your talk skeleton or hand out copies of it.
3 Use the frame to extol a 'new' product. (See the example talk on p. 81.) Here and there spice your talk with humour. Also, make a point of pausing now and then to look at the skeleton.
4 Deal with any questions.
5 Form the class into groups of six and assign everyone an object.
6 Hand out sheets of A4 paper and ask everyone to draw their object onto it large and bold. Add that their drawings will be their prototypes.
7 Allow time for students to make a few notes on what they are going to say, but do not let this phase last too long as it is not necessary for each talk to include the full number of points made in the skeleton. (Speakers often think up points once they begin talking.)
8 As the groups are ready, start them off, adding that in each group someone must introduce the first speaker by saying, for example, *Ladies and gentlemen, let's give our first speaker a warm welcome!*

Tips
• Give everyone a skeleton which even the least proficient learner can handle. (Proficient learners will tend to fill it in more fully and vary it without being told to.)
• Step 4: Point out that you did not memorise the discourse skeleton. Rather, you simply looked at it from time to time and read what was there, much like a speaker in a parliament might look occasionally at notes when speaking.

- Step 5: Allow students to speak about a different product from the one you have given them, but point out that devices which are (a) imaginary or (b) real but complex may be difficult to talk about in an interesting way. One reason for this is that, in the case of a fantasy invention, *all* the uses mentioned must be dreamed up on the spot.

Variations

- On the skeleton, mark a few phrases which everyone must use and leave unmarked certain other phrases which the more proficient can use if they want.
- Step 5: Form mixed-proficiency pairs (who then join to form groups of eight students). Partners prepare together. Say that in pairs they should decide how to divide up their presentation. For example, one student can read out the frame itself and, if they want, one or two of the points to be made, while the other supplies everything else. Almost invariably the least proficient student will take on an easier role.
- Students present other things, e.g. the virtues of their country, region or town as a tourist destination, or their street or neighbourhood as a good place to live.
- Create different skeletons for other types of presentation, e.g. give each student a copy of the same very blurred photocopy (which you can make by copying a coloured photo, then copying from the copy, and so on). Students, in turn, say what they see. Example skeleton: *OK, let me tell you what I see here. First of all, here is/are . . . I also see . . . And here I see . . . And, . . . Finally, here . . . Are there any questions? Any more? If there are no (more) questions, next is ....* Other things students can present in this same general way (but with somewhat different skeletons) include a blank sheet of paper representing a real, well-remembered photo which they have at home.

Comment

Discourse skeletons can be devised for a very wide range of speaking activities. In my experience they have the following advantages:

- They give visible indication of how a stretch of talk or writing should be organised for a particular exercise. In particular, they can be used to present expressions that are widely useful for beginning, ending and internally structuring discourse of a particular type.
- They strongly tend to enable one's least proficient students to speak more interestingly, more comprehensibly, and at greater length than they

otherwise would. Even one's most proficient students can get ideas from them.

- Seeing a skeleton tends to help everyone better understand the oral presentations which follow since the skeleton gives an idea of what kind of information will be where.

Acknowledgement

The last two variations come from John Morgan (in Lindstromberg, 1990, e.g. p. 47).

Pitching a wonderful new product – a skeleton

- Thank you for that inspiring welcome. Well, I'd like to begin by thanking you all for coming to this presentation of a wonderful new product.
- We have decided to call it the XXX.
- I'd like to tell you all about it. Afterwards, you will have an opportunity to ask about anything you like.
- The XXX is a truly tremendous advance.
- For one thing . . .
- For another . . .
- Additionally, . . .
- Also, . . .
- Plus, . . .
- Yet another great thing about the XXX is . . .
- What's more . . .
- And, as if that wasn't enough, . . .
- All in all, we believe the XXX is the wave of the future.
- I believe I have time to take three or four questions.
- If there are no (more) questions, I'll hand over to ....
- Thank you for your kind attention.

An example of how you might fill in the discourse skeleton

[Begin by holding up your *APPLAUSE!* card. Elicit the required warm welcome.]

- Ladies and gentlemen, *thank you for that inspiring welcome! Well, I'd like to begin by thanking you all for coming to this presentation of a wonderful new product.*
- *We have decided to call it the* pencil. [Display a pencil.]
- *I'd like to tell you all about it. Afterwards, you will have an opportunity to ask about anything you like.*
- *The* pencil *is a truly tremendous advance.*
- *For one thing,* you can write with it. You can even hold it upside down and it will not stop writing like the old-fashioned ballpoint pen will!
- *For another,* if you make a mistake, you can use this thing on the end to rub it out. We call this super hi-tech feature 'the rubber' or, for the American market, 'the eraser'.
- Additionally, the pencil is easy to sharpen if the writing end, or 'tip', becomes blunt. You can do this with any sharp knife, or with a special tool called a pencil sharpener, which I also plan to invent. You can even sharpen a pencil with your teeth if they are sharp enough and you are really desperate.
- *Also,* the pencil can be used for advertising! You can write your company name and website on the side, for example.
- *Plus,* you can play with a pencil. Like this. [Toss the pencil up in the air and catch it.] How better to pass the time on a boring plane flight from London to Australia?
- *Yet another great thing about the* pencil *is* that if you have two of them you can eat Chinese food, like this!
- *What's more,* pencils can be produced in any colour.
- *And, as if that wasn't enough,* you can use a pencil to kill a vampire such as Dracula.
- *All in all, we believe the* pencil *is the wave of the future.*
- *I believe I have time to take three or four questions.*
- *If there are no (more) questions, I'll hand over to ....*
- *Thank you* so much *for your kind attention.*

Seth Lindstromberg

3.14 Questions to the head

Age	11 and up
Level	Lower-intermediate–Advanced
Time	20 minutes
Focus	Interview-like dialogue, learning about empathy and role-switching
Material	A large portrait (photographs work best)

This interview–roleplay activity is a development of 'Picture interviews' (3.7). One difference is that one student is interviewed by the whole class. Another is that use of a 'mask' makes the interview–roleplay seem much more real.

Preparation

Choose a large portrait, preferably a photograph, of someone who you think might be interesting to your class on account of their age, physical features, clothing, setting and so on. Attach to the portrait a flap of paper of such a size and shape that the face is hidden but the hair and neck are visible.

Procedure

1 Hold up the masked portrait. Walk around and show it to the students, asking them to notice what they can about the hair, skin, clothing and so on.

2 Say that the person in the photograph is going to be a guest in the classroom.

3 Ask them each to prepare five to ten questions to ask this person when he or she arrives.

4 While most of the class are writing, choose a student who you feel has the ability to put her or himself in someone else's shoes. Ask this student (Student A) to come to the front of the class and then – hiding the portrait from the rest of the class – lift the mask and let Student A have a good look at the portrait. Tell everyone that Student A's job will be, when everyone is ready, to:
   • hide his or her face behind the portrait
   • pretend to be this person
   • answer questions from the class (e.g. *How old are you? Who are you? Where do you come from?*)

5 Leave this student at the front of the class to think about a life story while you check the questions that the others have been writing.

6 When everybody seems ready, say something like, *Well, everybody, we have a visitor today. Visitor, would you like to sit here at the front of the class? Now class, ask your questions.* Sit near enough to, but not directly beside, the 'visitor' in order to be able to help out, if necessary, by whispering ideas.

7 The interview begins.

Follow on
Everyone writes a paragraph about the visitor based on the interview.

Variations
- Write notes about the life history of the person on the back of their portrait so that, as students hide their face behind the portrait, they can look at the notes if they want.
- Use a portrait of a star likely to be popular with your group. But for this the student who speaks for the star must either know, or be given, key biographical information.

Acknowledgement
I learned this idea from Mario Rinvolucri and John Morgan.

Tessa Woodward

3.15 The third degree about a text

Age	14 and up
Level	Intermediate–Advanced
Time	30 minutes
Focus	Close reading, asking questions about a resource, answering questions in the limelight and under pressure
Material	A reading text, (variation) a number of question slips

Preparation
Choose a suitable reading text and make a class set of copies. Or use a text from your coursebook.

Procedure
1 Hand out copies of the text and ask students to read it and then, in groups of three, prepare a set of questions about the text which, later, will be asked to someone else in the class.
2 Bring the class together and find a fairly proficient student who is willing to occupy a seat at the front of the class. Or choose someone in an

unexpected way, e.g. choose the person with the longest hair, the whitest shoes or darkest clothes.

3 For the next three minutes the class fire questions at the person in the 'hot seat'.

4 When three minutes are up the old victim selects a new one. Continue until one person in each group has had a chance to answer questions.

Follow on

If you note down some of the questions asked during the activity, you can use them as examples in a short discussion of what makes an effective question.

Variation

Make a set of numbered slips each bearing a request for clarification or elaboration, e.g.

1 *In other words?*	2 *Could you say that again?*
3 *I would like to know more about that.*	4 *Why do you think that is true?*
5 *What is your evidence for that?*	6 *Could you say a bit more about that?*
7 *Could you elaborate?*	8 *I didn't really understand that.*
	© Cambridge University Press 2004

At the end of Step 1, distribute the slips to (especially) your quieter students. (Keep a record of who has what slip.) Explain that when you hold up one finger, whoever has Slip 1 must ask the question on it; when you hold up two fingers, whoever has Slip 2 must ask that question; and so on. Give your signals (during Step 3) at times when a question seems appropriate but no one is asking one.

Bonnie Tsai

3.16 Simulation and presentations by groups

Age	12 and up
Level	Intermediate–Advanced
Time	45 to 60 minutes
Focus	Moving from individual work to team work, speaking and listening
Material	Three excerpts from pop songs by different performers and/or class sets of photocopied blurbs from or about CDs

Preparation

You will need three short excerpts of music by different musical artists and/or photocopies of three different CD or album cover blurbs. Ideally, the musicians in question should be new to your students and should play music of a sort likely to appeal to your students.

Procedure

1   Ask students to work individually and write down all the vocabulary they know about the music business and to organise it under the following headings: *People* (e.g. *singer*), *Objects* (e.g. *CD*), *Places* (e.g. *record shop*), *Processes* (e.g. *making a recording*), *Genres* (e.g. *garage music*), *Motives* (e.g. *desire for fame*), *Adjectives* (e.g. *loud*).

2   In pairs, they help each other to expand and correct their own and each other's lists. (Note: Everyone needs to have their own list for later phases of this activity.)

3   Pairs combine to form groups of four. Tell the groups that they are record companies and each group/'company' has to think of (1) a name for their company and (2) a logo or picture and/or a slogan, and (3) they have to decide who is who in the company (e.g. managing director, recording engineer, talent scout, marketing manager, graphic designer).

4   Each company presents itself to the rest of the class by, for instance, displaying and explaining their logo and saying who is who.

5   Announce that all of their companies have, until about six months ago, been really successful with lots of Top 10 hits and awards but that things have not been so good in the last six months and they *really* need a new hit single or, better yet, album. Add that there are three new groups or solo artists on the music scene and that these three have been sending tapes and descriptions of their work to all the companies.

6   Either play short excerpts of music by different musical artists and/or hand out photocopies of three different CD or album cover blurbs. All the groups hear and/or see the same materials.

7   Tell the companies they now each need to decide which of the three (groups of) artists they want to offer a contract to.

8   When ready, the groups each explain their decision to the whole class.

9   (Optional) In any medium or large class, more than one company will have chosen the same artist or musical group so put record companies who have chosen the same artist together for a friendly business meeting. Say that the companies have become aware that the artist(s) in

question is/are trying to play one company off against the other in order
to get a huge fee. Tell them they should agree on a way to handle this
situation.

Follow on
The various conferring groups announce their decisions.

Variation
Work with a different topic/situation: the genetically modified (GM) food
industry, for instance. In Steps 1–2, first individually and then in pairs,
students compile ideas under the headings *People, Places, Processes,
Motives*. In Step 3, each group of four are top people in a GM food company.
They brainstorm and discuss according to the following brief: *Until about
six months ago your company was a great success. Now, bad news has come
in from researchers and from farmers. Crop yields are not up and each year
more and more herbicides are needed to control weeds. There are other
problems too. Environmentalists have been gaining support and of course
they are very much against GM crops. You decide that you need to put your
side of the story to the media more forcefully than ever before. What ideas
can you think of to convince people that the GM industry is a good thing?*
Next, students, still in their groups, all read articles for and against the GM
industry (go to, e.g. www.guardian.co.uk→ARCHIVE→keyword 'GM').
Then the members of each 'company' must decide whether to (a) change the
focus of their business by moving into new areas, (b) maintain the present
focus of their business but put more money into public relations, or (c) stay
in GM but put much more money into research. If they choose (a) or (c), the
members of each company should produce a blurb which summarises and
justifies their decision in as much detail as possible. If they choose (b), they
should produce an improved version of their earlier promotional blurb.
Finally, groups present their blurbs to the whole class.

Other topics/situations include: a newspaper or radio station or TV
programme (e.g. soap opera, news programme, quiz show) of a certain type
(students specify this) which recently began to lose readers/listeners/viewers;
a private school which no longer attracts as many students as before; a resort
which no longer attracts as many visitors.

Comment
Steps 1–4 are an instance of 'pyramiding', a class management method in
which students move from working alone, to working in pairs, to working in
groups of about four, with groups of four eventually presenting to other

groups or (as above) the whole class. At each stage there is a different task, but the tasks all relate to a single overall topic or theme.

Tessa Woodward

3.17 Performing stories from sounds

Age	12 and above
Level	Pre-intermediate–Advanced
Time	45 minutes
Focus	Discussion in groups, whole class discussion, (in higher-level classes) vocabulary for sounds, (follow on) narrative writing
Material	A recording of a sequence of evocative sounds, (optional) a screen behind which a small group of students can hide

Preparation

1 Record a sound story: a series of sounds such as glasses clinking, typing, and so on.
2 (Optional) Find something that can serve as a screen, e.g. an old sheet, enough clothes line to go from one side of the room to another and a few clothes pegs.

Procedure

1 Tell the class you will tell them a 'sound' story, with no words.
2 Play your recording.
3 In small groups students discuss what they think happens in the story.
4 Bring the class together and elicit ideas.
5 Form small groups and ask them to script and rehearse their own stories-in-sounds. While they are working, erect your screen, if you have one.
6 From behind a screen at the front of the class (or, if you have no screen, from the back of the class), the groups take turns presenting their stories-in-sound to the whole class.
7 After each presentation the audience speculates about what the sounds represented and check their guesses by asking the performers.

Follow on
Students each choose one of the stories and write it out in words, expanding on it as they like.

Variations
• Students record their stories on tape at home, and bring them for the next lesson.

87

- With high-level students, include some work on naming the sounds, e.g. *clinking, tapping, a swish*.

Acknowledgement

Alan Maley and Alan Duff have authored two useful books (with cassettes) on the use of sound stories in language teaching, *Sounds Interesting* and *Sounds Intriguing* (Cambridge University Press); both, sadly, are out of print.

Hanna Kryszewska

Mainly listening

Modern general English coursebooks are accompanied by audio cassettes or CDs (increasingly, video materials as well) which are generally quite good. You still may find, though, that the listening materials and/or the exercises that are part of a given unit in your book are not quite right for *your* class: perhaps the listenings are inappropriate in topic, too short, too long, too easy or too hard. Or, you may decide that the exercises fail to exploit the material sufficiently well; for instance, there may be inadequate provision for intensive listening or not enough carry-over into speaking. One purpose of this book is to offer a resource of supplementary activities that can be useful in such cases. As it happens, *all* of the activities in this collection involve *some* listening. But here you will find ones in which listening is particularly focused on.

Using your own voice

4.1 Ticking differences

Age	7 and up
Level	Elementary–Advanced
Time	10–15 minutes
Focus	Gist listening, speaking (accuracy)
Material	Photocopies of a single picture or a class set of a coursebook with pictures in it

Procedure

1   Give everyone a copy of the same picture or ask them all to look at a particular picture in their coursebook.

2   Tell them that you are going to talk about an imaginary picture that is similar to, but in some ways different from, the picture they are looking at.

3   Explain that they should listen to your description. Each time they hear something that is different from their picture, they should tick the relevant part of this picture. For example, if you say *The woman's hair is long*, but in their picture the woman's hair is short, they each tick her hair.

4 Ask students to tell you:
- what they ticked
- what you actually said

Follow on
In pairs, students take turns taking the role of teacher (as in Steps 3 and 4).

Variations
The basic idea of asking students to mark differences between a text they hear and something they see is almost infinitely transformable. For instance:

- Give students maps showing a route through the solar system, a continent, country, region, town, neighbourhood, park or house. Describe a route that deviates in a number of ways from the one shown.
- Students read a moderately easy text of 100–300 words. Then you read it to them out loud just a little bit faster than you ordinarily would if you were trying to be *perfectly* clear to students of their level. As you read, replace some words and phrases with synonyms; as you do so, they tick or underline the differences in wording. Finally, line by line, ask what they marked and ask who can remember what you actually said. Or they say what they remember in pairs.
- As above, except you interpolate words and phrases. Students mark where the interpolations were made. Finally, ask who can remember what you added where.
- As above, except you make changes of fact.

Seth Lindstromberg

4.2 General knowledge quizzes

Age	7 and up
Level	Elementary–Advanced
Time	10–20 minutes
Focus	Close listening, general knowledge
Material	A set of general knowledge questions

Preparation
Find or make a set of general knowledge questions. The Internet is a good source. Perhaps ask your students' other teachers (e.g. their geography teacher) to supply you with a few items that everyone should know the answer to by now.

Procedure

1 Say that everyone is going to participate in a general knowledge quiz – almost like on television – and divide the class into teams of five or six students each.

2 Give each team a name (or number) or ask each team to suggest their own name.

3 Explain how the quiz will work:
   - You will pose questions to each group in turn.
   - If Team 1 (for example) answers their question, they get three points.
   - If they cannot answer it, you ask the next team in the rota (which stays the same) until a team answers it. That team gets one point.
   - You will then ask Team 2 the next question, even if that team just got one point by answering a question that Team 1 failed to answer.
   - The winning team is the one which is the first to accumulate (for example) 15 points.

4 Begin the quiz.

Variations

- Make the teams larger, e.g. divide the class into halves. (This means that teams will not have to wait long for their turn; on the other hand, the likelihood increases that questions will be answered by the same few students each time.)

- Vary the way you represent the scores. For example, each team chooses a '*the* + adjective + noun' team name that must total (say) 15 letters, e.g. *The best guessers*. These names are written on the board. Each time a team wins three points, you circle three letters; and circle one letter each time they win one point. The winner is the first team to get all of its letters circled. Or, the team names are not written on the board to begin with. Rather, write the letters of the names on the board as points are won. For example, if a team gets three points, write up three letters of the team name. The winner is the team whose name is first to be written completely.

Seth Lindstromberg

4.3 Picture dictation – a basic version

Age	11 and up
Level	Lower-elementary–Advanced
Time	5–30 minutes
Focus	Listening, language for describing scenes, (follow on) speaking, reading and writing
Material	Blank sheets of paper, (follow on) pictures or photographs of simple scenes (for the speaking and writing work), a written description of a scene (for the reading work)

Preparation

Depending on the level of your learners, decide on the complexity of language you will use in describing a scene. The figure on the opposite page shows a few of the key categories.

Procedure (Pre-intermediate–Advanced)

1 On the board sketch a simple scene such as that shown on p. 93 and divide it as shown by the dotted lines.

2 Point to different people and things and elicit or teach how to say where they are and how to say whether people are standing or not and where they are facing.

3 Write a few key example sentences on the board (e.g. *There's a woman in the left foreground. She's sitting, facing right, and reading a book.*)

4 Ask everyone to copy the drawing and the example sentences.

5 Tell the class everyone needs a sheet of paper and that you are going to describe a scene which they must each draw. Add that they can look at the notes they have just made and encourage them to say things like *What was that again?* if they have not understood you.

6 Describe the scene. Circulate and repeat or adjust (parts of) your description as necessary to help everyone follow along.

7 Students look at each other's drawings.

Follow on

- Writing: Display another scene. Everyone writes a description of it. In lower level classes, this step will enable you to spot misunderstandings before the speaking activity described below. In higher level classes, writing can be done as homework. In this case you might ask your students each to describe a real scene such as a view they know well, or to describe a painting or photograph with which they are familiar.

- Speaking: Form pairs. In each pair one student gets a picture of a simple scene (well-chosen picture postcards are useful here). Student A describes her scene to her partner, B, who draws the scene. When finished, A shows her picture to B. Then B gets a picture which he should describe to her. (I have not had very good luck when I have asked students to draw their own scenes to describe to a partner. For example, there are always a few who draw a scene without perspective.)

Key language

- Spatial prepositions (to express the location of things with respect to each other): *behind the house, in the sky*
- Location both left to right and from near to far: *near us, in the (right) foreground, farther away, in the centre middle distance, in the distance, in the (left) background, in the (far) distance, on the left/right, in the centre*
- Orientation: *facing us, facing away from us, facing left/right*
- Position: Of people: *standing, sitting, lying (face down/face up/on her side), kneeling* Of things: *upside down, upright/right-side-up, lying on its side, lying on its back*

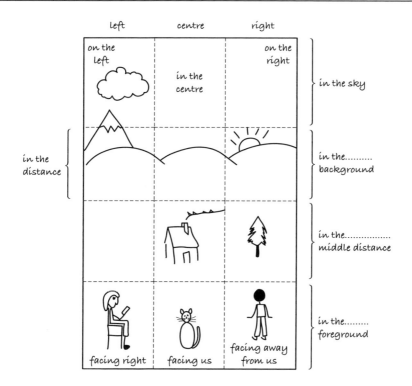

- Reading: Hand out a description of a scene. Students draw it. A variation is to hand out (corrected) descriptions written earlier as homework. Each student gets someone else's description. (If for any reason there are not enough suitable student-produced descriptions, just make multiple copies of one or more of the more interesting ones you did get.)

Variations
- After Step 4, erase the drawing from the board. Ask everyone to close their notebooks and then ask them what was in the drawing, where, oriented how, and so on.
- At elementary level, work with a narrow range of objects and prepositions, plus the phrases *near us, on the left, in the centre, on the right*.
- Describe the location of speech and thought bubbles (e.g. *Put a large speech bubble next to the girl*). Either dictate what is in them or ask students to fill them in as they like.
- With younger learners, mention colours and ask them to colour in their drawings accordingly.
- Ask students to add labels of various kinds. For instance, if you say *A suitcase full of dirty socks*, students each draw a suitcase and write the label *Full of dirty socks* or *F.o.d.s.*

Tip
As you describe a scene, occasionally ask someone who you see has understood to repeat what you have said. This helps the less proficient follow along.

Seth Lindstromberg

Using recordings

4.4 Which one was it?

Age	11 and up
Level	Elementary–Advanced
Time	5–10 minutes
Focus	Listening for prominent words and phrases, gist listening
Material	A recorded listening, (optional) class set of a handout

Preparation

1 Listen to the recording you are going to use and note down 8–20 or so prominent words or short phrases in the order in which you hear them.

2   For each one, think of a synonym or paraphrase which your students are likely to know. For instance, if you have noted down the phrase *the week after*, pair it with *the following week*. If this is not possible, think of a word or short phrase which is thematically related. For instance, if you have noted down *skier*, pair it with *snowboarder*.

3   Make a two-column list such that the item in the listening (e.g. *the week after*) is in one column and the item you dreamed up (e.g. *the following week*) is next to it in the other column. But mix things up so that the items that are really in the listening are not always in the same column.

4   If your list is short, plan to dictate it or write it on the board. If it is relatively long, consider producing a handout.

Procedure

1   Present your two-column list of items and tell your class how you made it.
2   Ask them to guess what the listening might be about.
3   Say that you are going to play the listening and that in each row they should tick the item they actually hear.
4   After playing the recording, ask which words they ticked.
5   Ask them to tell you everything else they know about the listening.

Follow on
Give them another listening task, e.g. a list of questions.

Seth Lindstromberg

4.5 Who said what, when and why – using film excerpts

Age	13 and up
Level	Pre-intermediate–Advanced
Time	10–20 minutes depending on the excerpt
Focus	Listening for specific utterances, gist listening
Material	An excerpt from a film or TV programme on video cassette or DVD and the equipment needed to show it, a film script excerpt (e.g. off the Internet), a class set of handouts

Preparation

1   Find an interesting 20–180-second-long bit of film which involves only a few characters of whom each, ideally, has about the same number of lines.

2   Transcribe the dialogue or find it on the Internet and download it. You are now ready to make a numbered list of short sentences or even just expletives (e.g. *Oh, hell!*) that the various characters say. Ten to twenty

items is generally about right. The beginning and end of such a list will look as follows:

1 Not now! Not ever!
2 I will if you will.

. . .

15 Oh, no!

3 Make sure the items on your list are in the order they are spoken. The learners' basic task will be to listen and later say who said which line.

Procedure

1 Quickly introduce the characters in the excerpt by showing a bit of it (sound off) and saying who is who, or elicit this information from anyone who has already seen the film. Add or elicit any other brief introductory comment you think might be helpful, e.g. what the setting is or why the characters have come together at this point in the story.
2 Hand out copies of the list of key utterances and give students time to read through them.
3 For each item on the list, ask if anyone can guess which character says it and why.
4 Tell the class you are going to (a) play the excerpt and (b) ask them afterwards who said what.
5 Play the excerpt straight through. Then check in the way you said you would except, additionally, ask such questions as, *And what was she doing when she said that?*, *Why did he say that, do you think?*, *What was said just before?*

Seth Lindstromberg

4.6 Where do these words go?

Age	11 and up
Level	Elementary–Advanced
Time	15–25 minutes
Focus	Intensive reading, fairly intensive listening, thinking about collocation
Material	Class sets of handouts of song lyrics, audio cassette/CD and player

Preparation

1 Choose a song suitable for the level of your class and type up the lyrics with double or triple spacing. Omit a number of content words (i.e. not

small grammar words) but *leave no gaps*: one word per line is about right. Make a class set of handouts.

2 Make up a jumbled list of the words you deleted. You can make a class set of these too or, if you prefer, put them on OHP transparency or just plan to write them on the board or dictate them later.

Procedure

1 In whatever manner, show or give everyone the word list and check that everyone understands and knows how to pronounce all the words.

2 Ask students to form pairs or threes. For each word on the list, ask them to think of (and write on their lists) at least one word that could come either before or after it.

3 Bring the class together and ask what they have written before or after each word.

4 Hand out your lyric sheets and say that you have deleted words without leaving gaps. Ask them to read through the lyrics and put a slash wherever they think one of the words on the list might have been deleted. Also, if they think they know just which word it was, they should write it in the margin near the line in question.

5 Ask them to go back into their pairs and threes and compare their ideas.

6 Bring the class together and tell them:
   a You are going to play the song.
   b As they listen, they should draw slashes (maybe in a different colour of ink) where the missing words ought to be.
   c If they have time, they can also write the missing word, or at least its first letter or two.

7 Again in pairs or threes, students compare sheets and try to agree about what word goes where.

8 Elicit answers from the whole class and then play the song again.

Acknowledgement

A basic element of the procedure comes from Holme (1991), p. 69.

Seth Lindstromberg

4.7 Interactive song dictation

Age	11 and up
Level	Elementary–Advanced
Time	20–25 minutes, generally
Focus	Intensive listening, writing, making requests (e.g. *Could you replay the last bit?*)
Material	One short song (the lyrics of which you know), audio cassette/CD and player

Procedure

1 Write something like the following on the board:
  a *Could you play back the last bit?*
  b *What does .... mean?*
  c *How do you spell ....?*
  d *What's the word after/before ....?*
  e *I'm totally stumped. What was the last line?*
  f *OK.*

2 Explain to your students that:
  - you are going to play a song and pause the recording after each line
  - each time you pause the recording, they should write what they have just heard
  - you expect them to use the expressions on the board
  - they may work singly, in pairs or in threes

3 Start playing the song.

Variations

- Make and distribute a worksheet which gives the first letter of each word, followed by a blank.
- If your class is large:
  - Choose six students and assign each of them one of the expressions (a–f). For example, assign (a) to Anna, (b) to Naomi and so on. Write each name after the appropriate expression so that everyone in the class can see it clearly.
  - Tell the class that if anyone wants you to carry out one of the requests or commands, they must call out the name of the person to whom you assigned that expression. For example, if they want you to play back the last line, they have to call out *Anna!* Then Anna has to say *Could you play back the last bit?* (and you play it back).
- Vary the phrases.

- Use this method in ordinary dictations you deliver yourself or which nominated students deliver to others in groups of three to five. (If the text being used is long enough, the role of 'dictator' can be shared around the group.)
- Give lower-proficiency students handouts that give the first letter of each word and, perhaps, any words or expressions they are unlikely to know.
- Do interactive dictations with recordings of other kinds of text (e.g. short newspaper articles) or with texts that you read out yourself.

Tips (for Step 3)

- In order to get students using the phrases on the board, you may at first have to point at an expression (*a*, for instance) and call out someone's name. Then, of course, carry out the request.
- While students are writing a line, move around and see who has got it right. To help less proficient students get it too, ask someone who you see has it right to say what they have written. (The result is a bit of student-to-student dictation – very helpful for weaker listeners.) Then play the line again. Or, if you are unable to move around much, from time to time ask, *Who is confident they got that last line right?* or *Who can read out all the lyrics so far?*

Comment

This is one of the simplest ways to use a song with lyrics that are not obscured by crashing drums and so forth. Songs from the 1940s and 1950s are often very good because they are more likely than newer songs to be clearly sung, relatively short and unrepetitive. A bonus is that the relevant CDs are often quite cheap. Interestingly, such songs may appeal to younger learners much more so than ones which were fashionable very recently but are now 'old'.

Some usable songs

- Lower-intermediate and up: *Sway* (Dean Martin); *It's Now or Never*, *One Night with You* (Elvis Presley); *Tennessee Waltz* (Patti Paige or Eva Cassidy), *It Doesn't Matter Anymore* (Eva Cassidy)
- Intermediate and up: *My Funny Valentine* (Chet Baker); *I Left My Heart in San Francisco* (Tony Bennett or Julie London); *Cry Me a River* (Julie London); certain Beatles songs, e.g. *I'll Follow the Sun, Yesterday, In My Life*; *Sweet Dreams of You, I Fall to Pieces, Crazy* (Patsy Cline); *The Tracks of My Tears* (Smokey Robinson and the Miracles); *The Great Pretender* (The Platters); *Smile* (Nat King Cole); *Imagine* (John Lennon or Eva Cassidy)

- Upper-intermediate–Advanced: Various classic songs such as *Some Day* (Fred Astaire); *Send in the Clowns* (Judy Collins); *Smoke Gets in Your Eyes* (The Platters or Bryan Ferry); *Stardust* (Nat King Cole or Willie Nelson), *Someone to Watch over Me* (Willie Nelson)

Seth Lindstromberg

Listening activities in other chapters (excluding students listening to each other)
1.6 (one version); 5.4 (song); 8.4 and 8.5 (students hear a poem read by you or played on an audio cassette/CD); 8.13 (rap)

5 Mainly reading

A typical contemporary general English coursebook is a good source of standard ideas on how to help students become better readers. In using such a book you are bound to come across a range of pre-reading and post-reading tasks as well as tasks for developing learners' proficiency in core sub-skills of reading such as scanning for specific bits of information, reading for gist, reading with attention to details of fact, reading for information that is implied or assumed and reading with attention to details of form. The six activities which make up the first part of this chapter each focuses on one or more of these popular sub-skills.

There are, in addition, a few areas on which coursebooks tend to focus less. One such area is bridging the gap between being able to read narrative silently and being able to deliver it competently (see 5.2 and 5.7–5.9).

All the activities which follow exercise skills besides that of reading, but in each the reading phase is prominent. And each, at some point, involves what is called an 'information gap'. In most, this is brought about through use of one of the most effective elements in the armoury of the communicative language teacher: the technique of the 'jigsaw' reading. The basic steps are worth reviewing here.

Basic steps of a jigsaw reading

1 Different students read either different texts or different parts of the same text.
2 They each answer comprehension questions on their text.
3 Students who have read the same text sit together and compare their answers. (You may give them the correct answers when they have finished this stage.)
4 Students who have read *different* texts, or different passages, sit together and tell each other what they have read.

For the sake of brevity, Step 3 is not always specified in those activities (in this chapter and elsewhere) which employ the jigsaw technique. Nevertheless, it is usually a good idea to include it, *especially* if some of your students are poor, or hasty, readers.

Reading tasks for authentic English

5.1 Mind-map the text

Age	12 and up
Level	Pre-intermediate–Advanced
Time	30 minutes
Focus	The study skill of organised note-taking
Material	A text that covers various aspects of a single topic

Preparation
Make a class set of a reading text, or use one from your coursebook.

Procedure
1 Tell your class the topic of the text.
2 (Re)introduce the method of mind-mapping by eliciting information relating to the topic and incorporating it into a mind-map on the board (see the example opposite).
3 Divide the class into pairs and ask them to copy and extend the mind-map.
4 Combine pairs into fours. They compare their mind-maps.
5 Bring the class together to pool ideas. As ideas come, add them to the mind-map on the board.
6 Ask the pairs to get back together.
7 Hand out copies of the text. Each pair should read the text and add what they learn from it to their mind-map.
8 Bring the class together and discuss their additions.

Example mind-map for the topic 'a beach'

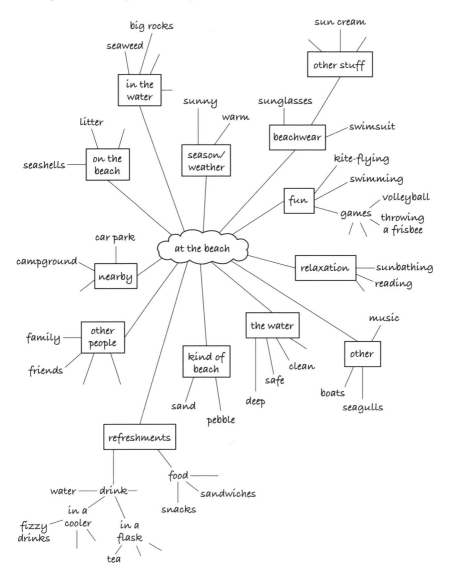

Tip

For more on mind-maps see Buzan (1995).

Hanna Kryszewska

5.2 Listening for the differences

Age	11 and up
Level	Intermediate–Advanced
Time	30 minutes
Focus	Listening for specific information, reading, reading aloud
Material	Multiple copies of fairly short texts (e.g. from newspapers)

Preparation

Collect and reproduce a series of short articles (about 200 words maximum) from English language newspapers or magazines.

Procedure

1 Divide the class into groups (of several students each) in which students may work either individually or as two-person teams.

2 In the groups, each student/pair gets a different article, which no one else must see.

3 They read it through and decide what are the ten most important details in the story (e.g. *last Monday, Mr John Brown, £397*).

4 They alter the story, changing those facts to, for example, *last Tuesday, Mr James Brown, £597*).

5 Give everyone in each group a copy of all the texts; they read them all through.

6 In turn, each individual or pair reads out their changed version twice. The listeners look at the corresponding original and follow along.

   a During the first reading, the listeners underline the differences they hear.

   b The listeners compare what they have underlined.

   c During the second reading, they write each difference at the side of the line where it occurs.

   d The listeners call out the differences they heard and the reader(s) say(s) whether they are correct.

   e If none of the listeners has the answer, the reader(s) read(s) out the relevant sentence again.

Comment

Step 6 can be spread out over two or more lessons.

Acknowledgement

This is related to an activity called 'Alternatives' in Michael Rost's brilliant book *Listening in Action* (1991).

David A. Hill

5.3 Put it in order

Age	13 and up
Level	Pre-intermediate–Upper-intermediate
Time	30–45 minutes
Focus	Reading, writing, speaking
Material	Three news-in-brief articles – class sets of two

Preparation

Find three news-in-brief articles that do *not* report events in strict chronological order. This should be fairly easy since most such articles are like this. One will serve as an example. Make a class set of each of the other two.

Example article

Police thwart hacker gang

Milan police have charged 14 minors with information piracy for hacking secret websites in Italy and abroad. Italian police said the sites included those of the US Army, NASA, and a firm specialising in computer firewalls. The hackers also broke into Italian websites, including that of the National Institute for Nuclear Physics.

© CAMBRIDGE UNIVERSITY PRESS 2004

Procedure

1   Display your example news-in-brief article on the board or via OHP and give your students time to read it.
2   Ask them what happened first, second and so on and write this on the board in brief form. Include *only* what the article explicitly mentions, e.g.

Hackers broke into Italian and foreign websites.
M. police arrested the hackers.
They charged h. with info piracy.

3   Ask them what happened between the items you have listed. In our example, that could be:

Hackers broke into Italian and foreign websites.
<u>*Someone contacted the police.*</u>

The police investigated.
They collected evidence.
M. police arrested the hackers.
They charged h. with info piracy.

4   Rub out everything but the verbs from the new version and ask your
     class (working individually or in pairs, as they like) to write the new
     version out in full and then tell it back to you.
5   Rub out the original version (or turn off your OHP) and ask them what
     information in the original version was missing from the new version. In
     our example, that would include the number of hackers and the sites
     that were hacked.
6   Hand out your other two articles: half the students (the As) get one
     article and half (the Bs) get the other.
7   Ask everyone to read their article and then, on a separate sheet of paper,
     note the events in time order. Ask them to include things that are
     explicitly mentioned and also things that are not mentioned but which
     must have happened. Add that:
     • they should not mention which is which
     • they can work in pairs if they like just so long as each person
       produces their own list
8   Students A and B swap both articles and lists of events.
9   Ask everyone (still in pairs) to:
     a read the other article and the list of events that goes with it
     b put an X in front of each event in the list that is not mentioned in the
        original article
     c see if they agree with the ordering of the events in the list
     d see if they can think of any other events that must have happened
        and decide where they should go in the list
10   Bring the class together and, for each article, elicit an ordered list of
     both mentioned and implied events.

Follow on

• Point out that stories written in strict time order:
     a have little or no need for the present perfect. In news-in-brief articles,
        on the other hand, a chronologically late happening may be told first
        with use of the present perfect in order to establish it as a recent
        occurrence of present relevance (as in the article given here).
     b have little need for the past perfect for the reason that the function of
        this tense is to signal a jump back in time. (The past perfect is used, for

instance, when narrative starts in the middle and then jumps to the beginning and then goes to the end.)

   c make heavy use of the simple past, a key narrative function of which is to indicate that events are in chronological order.

- Hand out other news-in-brief articles and ask students each to write a fully detailed new version in complete, chronologically ordered sentences.
- Upper-intermediate–Advanced: Give out/Elicit a synopsis of a well-known fairy tale such as *Cinderella* and ask them to rewrite it in the style of a typical short news article:

   a The headline is in the present simple: *Cinderella weds PC.*

   b The first sentence uses the present perfect to tell the end of the story: *Cinderella and her prince charming have married in his hilltop palace after a whirlwind courtship.*

   c The report then jumps back to the beginning of the story: *A mere week ago Cinderella, the stepdaughter of Mrs X, had to sleep next to the ashes in the fireplace . . .*

Tip

Step 7: The activity moves along much more smoothly if you tell your students they can write either very short sentences or phrases or even single words – provided that the sense is clear.

Seth Lindstromberg

5.4 Take a good song and make it better

Age	14 and up
Level	Intermediate–Advanced
Time	20 minutes
Focus	Intensive reading, a grammar focus (e.g. relative pronouns/clauses), (second variation) intensive listening
Material	A class set of the lyrics of a popular song; cassette/CD and player, (optional) a list of relative pronouns on a poster or OHP transparency

Preparation

1 Choose a song and format the lyrics with each line centred, like this:

Oh, when the saints
come marching in,
oh, when the saints come marching in . . .

107

This is to make it easier for students to add relative clauses into the lyrics, which is what they will be doing in Step 6.

2   Prepare a list of relative pronouns you want to review, e.g. *which, that, whom, where, when, how, why*. For quite proficient students, include ones such as *to whom, most of whom, of which, with which, at which point, since when, by when, by which time, someone that, anything that* and *those who*. If your list is long, prepare a poster or other means of displaying these items quickly during the lesson.

Procedure

1   Ask your students to form pairs.
2   Display/Write up your list of relative pronouns and elicit ways of using each one in a sentence. For instance, give your class a basic sentence like *The streets get hot* and ask them to expand in various ways by adding in relative clauses like this: *The streets where I live get hot* or *The streets get hot when July comes.*
3   Give out the lyrics and play the song.
4   Your students listen and mark where they think they could add in a relative pronoun. Add that:
   • they do not need to add in full relative clauses at this point
   • as a result of the eventual additions the song will no longer scan, but that they should not worry about that
5   (Optional) Play the song again.
6   In pairs, students add in as many full relative clauses as they can.
7   Working in groups of four, pairs compare their additions.

Variations

•   Other word classes to focus on include: adjectives; adverbials (point in time, duration, frequency, manner); expressions referring to sight, sound, feel, smell and movement; clause qualifiers (e.g. *luckily, perhaps, if I feel like it*); expressions of definiteness (e.g. *certainly, certain to*) along with ones of uncertainty (e.g. *maybe*) and vagueness (e.g. *sort of*).

•   (1) Choose a song your students probably do not know well. (2) Find and delete a few items of the same class (e.g. relative clauses that can be removed without affecting grammaticality). (3) Produce and distribute a class set of your altered, centred lyric handouts. (4) As described in the main procedure, ask students to add as many relative clauses (for example) as they can within a set time (between 5 and 10 minutes) and then compare what they have done. (5) Tell students to listen for the clauses you took out but not to write them down. (6) Play the song. (7) From memory, they try to add the clauses into the lyrics. (8) Play the song one more time. Congratulate especially anyone who managed to put in one of the exact phrases you had deleted.

Comment
- This is a good follow on when students have already listened to a song and filled in blanks in lyrics, but you can also use a song your students have never heard before.
- *California Dreaming* by The Mamas and The Papas is a good song for this activity.

Hanna Kryszewska

5.5 Quiz with a difference

Age	12 and up
Level	Elementary–Advanced
Time	15 minutes
Focus	Speaking, reading (of quiz items)
Material	Copies of a general knowledge quiz

This activity begins as a standard general knowledge quiz but abruptly transforms into a group problem-solving activity which gets students thinking about the assumptions behind test questions. It follows on from 'General knowledge quizzes' (4.2).

Preparation
Compose or find a general knowledge quiz. (The Internet is a good source.) Make any necessary photocopies.

Procedure
1 Set the quiz and ask everyone to answer the various items as usual.
2 Stop the students after two minutes, tell them you have changed your mind and divide them into pairs or small groups.
3 Ask them to write their *own* answers to some, or to all, of the questions. Their new answers must still be true, but they need not be the answers expected by whoever wrote the quiz. Indeed, it is better if they are not. For instance, to the question *Who was the first president of the United States?*, good answers would be:

a white man
a politician
a man
somebody who once lived in the English colonies

4 Students compare and comment on their answers.

Variation

Give each group a different quiz question. Ask them to write a true (but unexpected) answer on a slip of paper. Make sure the original question is not written on the slips. Redistribute the answers. Students decide what the original question might have been. (In the end, everyone sees the whole quiz.)

Hanna Kryszewska

5.6 Horoscopes

Age	15–16
Level	Intermediate–Advanced
Time	45 minutes
Focus	Reading for specific information, discussion, (follow on/variation) writing
Material	Pages with illustrations of the signs of the zodiac plus names and dates, descriptions of the basic characteristics of each sign, a set of week-old horoscopes

For students who know each other well.

Preparation

1 Collect a small picture (plus name and dates) of each sign of the zodiac and put them all on a sheet of A4 paper.
2 Collect general descriptions of people born in the 12 star signs as well as a week-old prediction for each sign. Put each description on a different sheet of paper.
3 Decide how to do Step 1 below.

Procedure

1 Elicit the signs of the zodiac, write them up in order on the board, and add the dates next to the names.
2 Ask who is what sign.
3 Hand out the sheet bearing the names and dates of the signs.
4 Form groups, with each group consisting of students of the same sign and

ask them to try to write a list of what they think are the typical characteristics of their sign. They can do this in two ways:
- by drawing on whatever lore of signs they already know
- by finding out what characteristics they have in common

5 When the lists are ready, give out the sheets with the general characteristics on. Ask them to compare/contrast the ideas on their lists with the official characteristics.

6 Ask them to remain in their groups and discuss the main things that happened to them during the week before. They should try to find a pattern within their group, and agree on its main elements.

7 Give each group a copy of the previous week's horoscope for their sign to compare with their thoughts from Steps 4–6.

8 Ask the 'sign groups' to break up so that students sit in pairs or threes with someone they know very well who is *not* from their original sign group.

9 Ask everyone to read the text on the characteristics of their friend's sign, decide how true it is about their friend, and say things like *It says that Virgos are usually very tidy, but you are very untidy!*

Follow on

For homework, students write about their views on horoscopes and/or how true the general information you provided is about themselves (using the language of comparison and contrast).

Variations

- In Steps 5–7, students put their thoughts down in writing.
- Begin the lesson by eliciting various ways of comparing things and, if appropriate, say that they will have opportunities to use some of them in the lesson to come.

David A. Hill

Students read out or tell stories

5.7 Reading aloud

Age	7 and up
Level	Lower-elementary–Advanced
Time	15–20 minutes
Focus	Pronunciation, measured delivery of a written text, dramatic reading, awareness of sentence and phrase structure, (optional) consideration of what makes a good storyteller
Material	A prepared text, (optional) a class set of photocopies of it

This activity is important preparation for other storytelling activities (e.g. 3.9, 3.17, 5.8, 5.9).

Preparation

1 Type out a text in a way that indicates where someone who is reading out loud would pause if reading *deliberately and dramatically*. (See the example on p. 114.) One way of doing this is to start a new line wherever one might pause for breath or for dramatic effect. In principle almost any kind of text will do. The example is a simplified news-in-brief article.

2 Prepare a class set of photocopies (or dictate the text, or display it on the board or via OHP).

Procedure

1 On the board, write a few brief pre-questions (or dictate them): *When?*, *Where?*, *Who did what?*, etc.

2 Read the text out deliberately and dramatically. Be sure to pause *distinctly* at the end of each line.

3 Elicit answers to the questions you posed.

4 Ask if anyone remembers anything else about the story.

5 Hand out (or display) the text and allow time for reading.

6 Ask everyone to put one loop around each of the sentences and to mark every punctuation mark in some manner (e.g. with a highlighter pen or a little pencilled circle).

7 Tell them:
   • *Make a long pause at the end of each line.*
   • *Make a* very *long pause at each comma or dash.*
   • *Change your voice at each quotation mark.*
   • *Make a* very, very, very *long pause at the end of each sentence.*

8 Lead choral, and a bit of individual, repetition of bits you think may pose pronunciation problems. Also, ask if anyone would like to practise any other parts of the text.

9 Explain how to read sub-vocally: that is, a person reads the text, thinks it, moves their tongue and lips (and may even gesture), but does *not* make a sound.

10 Tell everyone to read the text sub-vocally once.

11 Tell them to number their loops. (In the example on p. 114, that would be *1, 2, 3, 4*.) Add that they are going to read the story out around the class again and again until everyone has read exactly one sentence. Make sure everyone knows what order he or she is supposed to go in.

12 Start the sequential reading. Interrupt and give guidance whenever someone has not paused long enough.

13 Ask the class to pair up (or form threes) and read out alternate sentences, *with pauses*. Ask them to do this two or three times with a different student beginning the story each time. Circulate and give students feedback, especially about use of pausing and other dramatic techniques such as changing voice at quotation marks.

Tip
Step 13 is more interesting if the text is somewhat longer than the example given here.

Variations
- Before the main sequence, elicit thoughts about the characteristics of a great storyteller and write them on the board (and/or nominate a couple of students – one of your friendship pairs (see p. 22) perhaps – to represent these thoughts on a poster that can be stuck up on a wall). One way of generating contributions is to show a short film excerpt in which a good actor tells an anecdote well. Here are a few things that might come up: expressive use of the face and hands, changing the voice and stance for different characters, variation in speed with lots of dramatic pauses, considerable variation in pitch, involving the listener by making eye contact and asking questions, good use of visual aids and props. Then say that they are going to practise some of these skills.
- Arrange the lyrics of a song in the way shown on p. 114. After working with the text as described above, play the song. Afterwards, ask everyone to hide their lyrics and to call out all the phrases they can remember. (Perhaps give them a couple of minutes first to write some down.)
- Use a text which is at the level of your least proficient students (though they should be at lower-elementary level at least). Even with a relatively easy text, higher-level students generally find sufficient challenge in trying to improve their ability to read *dramatically*.

Sample text (Pre-intermediate)

Police in the **USA**
　　　arrested a man for **deal**ing **drugs**.
They **hand**cuffed him
　　　and began to **put** him
　　　　　in their **car**.
Saying,
　　　　　'I don't want to go to **jail**',
　　　　　　he tried to **bite** the car.
As a re**sult**,
　　　he not only had to go to **jail**
　　　　　but he **al**so
　　　　　　had to pay $200 **extra**
　　　　　　　for **scrap**ing
　　　　　　　　a 12-inch **gash**
　　　　　　　　　in the **paint**
　　　　　　　　　　with his **teeth**.

© CAMBRIDGE UNIVERSITY PRESS 2004

Seth Lindstromberg

5.8 What comes next?

Age	9 and up
Level	Pre-intermediate–Advanced
Time	15–30 minutes, up to 40 minutes the first time you do this
Focus	Intensive reading, reading aloud, good oral delivery of a written text, basic storytelling skills (e.g. involving your audience, use of gesture, not telling a story too quickly), getting students to pay close attention to what each other says
Material	Class sets of stories

This oral accuracy activity is particularly useful in monolingual classes where students have a tendency to lapse into their mother tongue when doing pairwork. It is generally a good idea to do Activity 5.7 at least once before attempting this one which, itself, is good preparation for 5.9 and any freer student-to-student storytelling activity.

Preparation

1   Find a story which is likely to be interesting to your students. In terms of grammar and vocabulary, it should present little or nothing that is completely new. Ideally, the story should be no longer than two sides of A4 paper, double-spaced. The story given on p. 118 is one which some students will already know; this does not matter and can even be an advantage in lower-level classes.

2   Read the story out loud as dramatically as you can manage. Then mark places in the story where, if you pause while reading it out, your students have a good chance of guessing the rest of a word or the word that comes next. Suppose, for instance, your story begins:

   a   *Once upon a time, a long long time ago, there was a beautiful princess who lived in a castle made of black stone with her parents, the king and queen.*

   In (b), double slashes show *good* places to pause:

   b   *Once upon a // time, a long long time // ago, there was a beautiful // princess who lived in a // castle made of black // stone with her par//ents, the king and // queen.*

   In (c), the double slashes show *bad* places to pause:

   c   *Once upon a time, a long long time ago, there was a // beautiful princess who lived in a castle // made of black stone // with her parents, the king and queen.*

3   Make a class set of the same story with marks (e.g. double slashes) showing good places to pause. Students will work mostly in A/B pairs so, typically, the first half of the story should be on one sheet and the second half on another.

Procedure

1   Read the story out to the class, pausing where you have made marks.
   • Try to read it out as much as possible as if you were telling it from memory.
   • Make it clear (e.g. by look and gesture) that whoever has an idea should call out what they think is coming next.
   • If a contribution is not correct, give a hint such as, *Right meaning, wrong word* (e.g. if someone says *rock* instead of *stone*), *Almost* (if someone says *palace* instead of *castle*), *No, younger* (if someone says *queen* instead of *princess*). However, do not drag things out too much. If you do not get the right word after about six seconds, supply the word and continue with the story.

- It is *very* important that you use gesture as much as possible even for words you are not expecting students to guess, e.g. if you say *grabbed*, mime grabbing.
- Echoing correct guesses makes this activity work much less well. So, if a student correctly calls out *Princess* try *not* to continue as follows: *Princess who lived* . . . Either just continue *who lived* . . . or say *Yes!* . . . *who lived* . . . This is because one thing you want to demonstrate is how the listener can participate in telling the story. A teller who echoes works against this aim. (If a student speaks too quietly, ask them or another student to repeat the word.)

2 When you have finished telling the story, check that everyone has got the gist.

3 Ask them to show you some of the gestures you made and see if they can say what each gesture represented.

4 Ask if they can recall other ways in which you helped them to guess what was going to come next.

5 Say that they, in pairs, are going to take turns doing what you just did.
- Explain the significance of the marks in the story sheets they are about to get.
- Remind them about the six-second time limit after which the speaker should just say the word their partner was supposed to guess.

6 Hand out the story sheets and give everyone enough time to read their part. Then start the pairwork. (In general, your least proficient students should get the first part of the story.)

7 As students finish, give everyone the half of the story they did not get initially.

Follow on

Ask early finishers to write, from memory, three sentences: one from the beginning of the story, one from the middle and one from the end. (Anyone who finishes really quickly can, of course, write even more sentences.) As you circulate, look especially at what your least proficient students are writing. Try to remember some of their sentences. When most of the class have written at least three sentences, ask if anyone has written a good first sentence for the story. Ask him or her to read it out. Ask if anyone has a good second sentence, and so on. Call on one of your least proficient students at any point in the story for which you know they have an appropriate sentence. (Lead this plenary storytelling as briskly as possible.)

Variations
- If you have an odd number of students, create one or more A/BB threesomes. The two Bs read out alternate sentences or paragraphs in their part of the story.
- In later lessons, give students a pre-marked story that you have not read out before.
- Use two *different* stories or short anecdotes. (Neither story should be much longer than one A4 side of paper with 1.5 line spacing.)
- Give students *unmarked* texts. They add the slashes. This is a very interesting intensive reading activity which requires each student to think about what is likely to be comprehensible to their partner. Add that after they have gone through the story, everyone should give their partner some brief feedback on his or her placement of pauses, e.g. *The hardest for me to guess was . . . An easy one was . . .*
- If your room has poor acoustics or if your class is very large and a bit unruly, experiment with more teacher-centred versions:

LARGE MIXED ELEMENTARY AND PRE-INTERMEDIATE/ INTERMEDIATE CLASSES

Do all the reading yourself. Divide the class into mixed ability teams and award points to each team for its correct guesses.

LARGE MIXED PRE-INTERMEDIATE AND INTERMEDIATE CLASSES

Divide the class into two or three teams. Give the members of each team a different part of a text with slashes already in. For example, half your class get the beginning of the story and the other half the end. (If they have not read the text before, give them time to read it now. Again, if the text is new, it should be easy in terms of vocabulary and, especially, grammar.) Ask for volunteer readers from each group. The readers from Group A (in turn) read out their part of the story with pauses. At each pause, call out a row number. Any Group B student sitting in that row can guess what word comes next. Then readers from Group B read out the last part of the text. You can spice this up by awarding groups (or rows) a point for each word they guess.

Acknowledgement
Part of the idea for this activity comes from Holme (1991), pp. 48–9.

Example text (Pre-intermediate–Intermediate)

The stupid monkey

One day Ann was out walking, just for exercise. Near the entrance to a park she saw a small crowd of people standing in a // circle. They were looking at something. She crossed the street to get a better // look.

In the middle of the circle, or ring, of people there was an old woman and a monkey. That's what everybody was looking // at. On the ground near the mon//key was a hat. It was upside down. The woman wanted the monkey to do a trick but the monkey did nothing. It just sat there on the // ground. Perhaps this monkey was very stu//pid. Or maybe it just did not want to do any // tricks. The old woman shouted at the monkey more and more // loudly. Suddenly, the monkey stood on its back legs, screamed and fell // over.

The woman went near it. She bent over the monkey. It did not move. She called its name. It still did not // move. She touched it tenderly, whispering its name one more // time. The old // woman got down on her // knees. She put her ear against the monkey's chest and // listened. Then she whispered, 'He's dead!' and began to // cry. From time to // time she said again, 'Dead. Dead. My only friend. What will I do // now? How will I live without my // monkey?'

A young man stepped towards the hat, took a five-pound note out of a // pocket and dropped it in the // hat. He turned to the crowd and said, 'We have to help // her. Can't you see, her life is ruined.' He then walked // away.

Other people began to move towards the // hat, taking notes and // coins out of their pockets and // handbags and dropping them in. Ann did the // same.

Several months later, Ann was in a different city, on bus//iness. One lunchtime, she decided to go for a // walk. It was a beautiful spring day and she could see on her map that there was a park nearby. She decided to buy a // sandwich and eat // it on a bench in the // park. About ten minutes later she got to the park entrance. Near it was a crowd of people looking // at something. Ann joined // them. In the middle was an old woman and a // monkey. Near them was an upside down // hat.

It was the same woman and the // same monkey. Again the monkey screamed and // fell over. Again the woman // cried. Again a young man // stepped forward and put // money in the // hat and spoke to the // crowd. It was the same hat. And the same // young man. © CAMBRIDGE UNIVERSITY PRESS 2004

Example text (Intermediate)

Showing respect (Traditional: the Middle East)

Nasradin Odzha was a judge. One morning, on his way to the courthouse, he smelled coffee as he passed by a // café. He decided to go // in. By the way, it is important in this story that Mr Odzha usually dressed very simply, like a peasant – you know, like an ordinary small farmer. Anyway, he went into the // café and greeted the men sitting here and // there in the café. But! Nobody answered his // greetings! Mr Odzha said to himself, 'Oh, this won't do! I can't have this! I have to teach them how to behave.' So, he went // home and put on a new fur coat – the most expensive coat he owned – and // returned to the // café. He greeted the men and they greeted him back. One of them called to the owner of the // café, 'Make a cup of // coffee for Nasradin Odzha!'

After a bit, the coffee was brought to Nasradin Odzha. He took his cup and poured the coffee all over his // coat. The other customers shouted, 'Hey, Mr Odzha, what did you do that // for? We treat you to coffee, and you pour it all over your //coat!'

Judge Odzha said, 'Well, you paid my coat more respect than you paid to // me so I thought my coat deserved to have the // coffee.'

© CAMBRIDGE UNIVERSITY PRESS 2004

Seth Lindstromberg

5.9 Imagine that!

Age	11 and up
Level	Pre-intermediate–Advanced
Time	25–40 minutes
Focus	Intensive reading and listening, reading aloud, good oral delivery of a written text, the storytelling skills of involving your audience and not telling a story too quickly, getting students to pay close attention to what each other says
Material	Class sets of a story

Here, each student reads out part of a story and also asks the questions that are embedded in it. The ones who are listening have to listen intently and give plausible replies by using their imagination. In so doing, they help tell the story.

Preparation

Photocopy your story so that the first and second halves are on different sheets (or different sides of the same sheet) and make a class set of each half.

Procedure

1 Form pairs and hand out the story sheets so that the students in each pair get different halves of the story. Give everyone time to read the story and ask questions about pronunciation, vocabulary and so on.

2 Explain that in each pair the person with the first part of the story should read not only the story but also the questions that are embedded in the text. Add that the other person in the pair puts down his or her part of the story, listens and answers any questions the teller asks. Stress that listeners must *use their imagination*. Start them off.

Variations

• If you have an odd number of students, form a threesome. Fold their sheets so that they each see a different third.

• Between Steps 1 and 2, put students who have read the same (half) story together in groups of three or four. Each group should include at least one relatively proficient learner. Give each group some comprehension questions to look at. They try to agree on the answers. Mingle and help out. Next, still in their groups, students rehearse reading their part of the story.

• At Step 2, add facetiously that there is no point in them torturing each other. How can they avoid doing this? They must read out their parts of the stories *as interestingly as they can*. Elicit things storytellers do in order to tell a story in an interesting way. (5.7, 'Reading aloud', could be done before this activity; if so, remind your class of what they learned in doing it.)

Example story (Intermediate–Advanced)

The appointment

Once upon a time, about a thousand years ago, there was a powerful caliph in Baghdad. He had a great many servants in his palace. [WHAT KINDS OF JOBS DID HIS SERVANTS DO, FOR EXAMPLE?] Among these servants was a man named Abdul. He was the caliph's favourite servant. [WHY WAS HE THE CALIPH'S

(continued)

FAVOURITE?] He helped the caliph to get dressed and also made his coffee. And then he always tasted it before giving it to the caliph. [WHY DID HE TASTE THE CALIPH'S COFFEE BEFORE THE CALIPH DRANK IT?] [ALSO, WHAT OTHER JOBS DO YOU THINK HE DID FOR THE CALIPH?]

One morning, the caliph wanted some fruit, so he asked Abdul to go to the central market and get several different kinds of really fresh, ripe fruit. [WHAT KINDS, FOR EXAMPLE?] Abdul got a basket from the kitchen and set out for the market. It was still early morning but Abdul could see that it was going to be a really hot day. [WHAT MADE HIM THINK SO?]

He walked through the narrow streets of the old part of the city. Soon, he was in the market. [WHAT DID HE SEE ON HIS WAY?] [WHAT DID HE HEAR?] The market was already thronged with shoppers. [WHAT DO YOU THINK *THRONGED* MEANS? (ANSWER: 'CROWDED')] [WHAT WERE THE SHOPPERS WEARING?]

Abdul walked past piles of shoes, past chickens, past ducks, past bags of rice, past pots, past chairs until, finally, he got to the part of the market where they sold what he was looking for. [DO YOU REMEMBER WHAT HE WAS LOOKING FOR?]

Carefully, he looked over every piece of fruit. [WHY?] If he saw some fruit that looked good, he felt it to see if it was hard or soft. He looked at it especially carefully to see if there were any rotten, brown bits. He also smelled each fruit. [WHY DID HE SMELL EACH FRUIT?] He bought some golden yellow melons and some fragrant green ones. He bought some oranges and fresh figs. Soon, his basket was almost full. [HE DECIDED TO GET ONE MORE KIND OF FRUIT . . . WHAT WAS IT, DO YOU THINK?]

Suddenly, he felt like someone was watching him from behind. He turned around. About five metres away was a tall man dressed completely in black. The man's eyes were hidden inside a large black hood. Abdul could see only one part of his face. [WHICH PART WAS THAT?] Suddenly, Abdul was very, very afraid. Abdul could not see the man's eyes, but he felt the man staring at him. [HOW WOULD YOU FEEL IN THIS SITUATION?]

'What do you want?' Abdul asked. The man in black did not answer.

'Who are you? What do you want?' shouted Abdul. [WHY DID HE SHOUT?]

After a long silence . . . the tall man in black said . . . v e r y slowly . . . in a deep voice, 'If you must ask . . . I . . . am . . . **Death**! . . . **Your** death!'

This answer shocked Abdul. He dropped his basket and ran back to the palace as fast as he could. He ran into the caliph's meeting room and threw himself on the floor at the caliph's feet. [WHAT DO YOU THINK HE IS GOING TO SAY?]

(continued)

'Oh, Master!' he said, his voice shaking with fear. 'Please let me leave Baghdad immediately. Please let me go to my brother's house in Basra. Please let me stay there.' [WHAT IS 'BASRA'? (ANSWER: A DIFFERENT CITY)] Abdul added that he had just had a terrible shock and needed some peace and quiet.

The caliph could see that Abdul was very upset [WHAT MADE THE CALIPH THINK THIS?] and so he said, 'Yes, you may go.' And so Abdul set off for Basra, a city south of Baghdad. [HOW DID HE TRAVEL, DO YOU THINK?] [WHAT WAS HE THINKING ABOUT AS HE MADE HIS WAY SOUTH?]

The caliph, though, wanted to find out about the tall stranger in black. And so, with a bodyguard, he went to the market. [SAY THREE THINGS ABOUT THE BODYGUARD.] The man in black was not hard to find. [WHY NOT?] The caliph's bodyguard told the man to stop and not move. The caliph began to ask him questions. [WHAT WERE SOME OF HIS QUESTIONS?] One question he asked was, 'Why did you frighten my servant?'

The man in black replied, 'Who is your servant?'

'His name is Abdul', said the caliph. 'And he . . .' [CAN YOU DESCRIBE ABDUL IN DETAIL?]

'Oh, yes. I remember now,' said the stranger. 'But I did not mean to frighten him; that was not my intention. I stared at him only because I was surprised to see him here in Baghdad.'

'And why is that?' asked the caliph.

'Because . . .' said the man in black, 'I have an appointment with him tonight. [AN APPOINTMENT WHERE, DO YOU THINK?] Our appointment is in Basra!'

Said the caliph, 'Poor Abdul. Poor, poor Abdul.'

[WHAT IS GOING TO HAPPEN TO ABDUL? WHAT DO YOU THINK THE MORAL OF THIS STORY IS?]

Comment

Most stories will require some introduction. In this case, it is normally helpful to find out what the class know about Baghdad. *Where is it? What is the climate like? How was life there different some twelve hundred years ago?* And so on. Some vocabulary may need pre-teaching too: *caliph* and *the moral of a story*, for instance.

Seth Lindstromberg

Reading activities in other chapters ('PR' = post-reading activity)
1.6, 1.8, 1.9, 3.15 (PR), 4.1 (second variation), 4.6, 6.9, 7.1, 8.4–8.6, 8.8–8.15

Mainly writing

Teachers generally accept that students should speak, listen and read in class. The same is not true of writing. Many teachers are wary of devoting precious class time to development of this skill. I believe though that it can be useful practice to have your students write at least a few sentences in almost every lesson. As long as this written work is properly guided and truly short, and is not utterly mechanical, the reading and correction you end up doing will be well worth the time you spend. How could I persuade a doubter?

Properly chosen in-class writing activities have the following advantages:

a   Good writing tasks get learners using their English to communicate to others and/or to express themselves creatively; either can be very motivating.

b   Writing gives students time on their own to have and to develop their thoughts.

c   It can, therefore, create a beneficial time of quiet where all are working simultaneously on a beneficial task.

d   Written work gives you hard evidence of level and progress. Furthermore, the products of *good* writing tasks enable you to get to know your students' thoughts. Of course you have to look at the written work to gain this advantage, or listen to students reading it out.

e   Looking at what students write opens up an avenue for building good relations with individual learners. That is, you can include, where appropriate, conversational replies to what students have written. (e.g. *That must have been a real shock to you! I hope you feel better now.*)

f   If you generally collect or inspect their work, students feel more monitored which may make it easier to maintain order.

g   Some writing tasks result in student-produced material that you can use to generate interesting and well-structured student-to-student talk as in, for instance, 'ABC sentences' (6.2, p. 4 and pp. 125–126) and 'Write in the shape' (6.8, p. 10 and pp. 135–137).

In the activities that follow, writing phases are particularly prominent, although other skills are focused on as well.

6.1 What's the number?

Age	11 and up
Level	Elementary–Advanced
Time	15 minutes
Focus	Writing phrases or sentences, awareness of how word meanings can be exemplified
Material	Sheets of paper, bilingual dictionaries
Function	Closer

Procedure

1 Divide students into small groups and give out one sheet of paper per group. Suggest they get their dictionaries ready.
2 Tell the groups each to choose a number between 0 and 10 and keep it a secret.
3 On their sheet, group members write a total of three riddle-like phrases or sentences which hint at the number they have chosen. For example, if they have chosen 4, they might write:

A dog has this number of legs.
The number of instruments in a quartet.
.... wheels on a car.

Make sure no group writes the actual number on their sheet.
4 Each group passes its sheet to another group, one of whose members reads out what is written on it. They all then try to agree (in whispers) what the secret number is.
5 To show they have correctly recognised the number, students add two more similar hinting phrases onto the list they have received.
6 The sheets are passed to new groups and the procedure is repeated (and repeated) until each sheet returns to the group that began it.
7 Each group chooses their favourite riddles.
8 Groups read their favourite riddles out to the rest of the class.

Follow on
Place the finished lists in a self-access corner of the class, or exhibit them on the wall. (But first correct them, even perhaps type them up.)

Variations
• In Step 2, allocate numbers to groups yourself, if you want to avoid different groups sharing the same number.

- Instead of passing on their sheets to another group, each group in turn calls out their three riddles. Every other group confers and prepares a phrase that hints at the number in question. For example, if the number was 4 and a group's phrases were:

Legs a dog has.
The number of instruments in a quartet.
Wheels on a car.

Then other groups read out their just-written hints for the same number:

The number of legs of a typical table.
The .... corners of a square.
An octopus that has lost four tentacles.

For this variation, students need to cooperate within their teams. Add an element of competition *among* teams by awarding teams points for a riddle that is factually correct (1 point) and grammatically correct (1 point).
- Instead of numbers, start with nouns or adjectives, for example *dog*. Then students might write:

    It's man's best friend. It has four legs. It doesn't like cats.
    Or, if the word is *blue*:
    The colour of the sky. The colour of the sea on a fine day.
    Or, if it is *spaghetti*:
    It's long. It's white. They eat it in Italy.

Hanna Kryszewska

6.2 ABC sentences

Age	11 and up
Level	Elementary–Advanced
Time	15–30 minutes
Focus	Accuracy in writing, listening to others
Function	Ice-breaker, closer

Procedure
See p. 4.

Variations
- Down the left side of their paper students write a word or phrase, e.g. one denoting a topic such as *high fashion*. Following the rules on p. 4, they write sentences which have a connection with the topic.

- Students list numbers instead of letters. Sentence 1 must contain the word *one* (e.g. *There is only one sun*), Sentence 2 must contain the word *two* (e.g. *I have two thumbs*) and so on.
- Make the activity more difficult by telling them that the *first word* of the sentence has to begin with the 'target' letter.
- The activity becomes easier if the letter can come anywhere in the sentence (e.g. *I waShed my face this morning*).

Comment

On first impression it may seem that a very restrictive frame of rules such as in this activity or 'Write in the shape' (6.8) must restrict creativity. In fact, such frames do the opposite, which is a prime reason why traditional forms of poetry such as the rhyming couplet, the sonnet, the limerick and the haiku have remained popular with people wishing to express themselves creatively. For more 'frame-governed' writing activities, see 8.1–8.3. (See also Holmes and Moulton, 2001.)

Acknowledgement

I learned the core idea from Hanna Kryszewska in a workshop she led at Pilgrims Language Courses.

Seth Lindstromberg

6.3 Writing from a medley

Age	14 and up
Level	Pre-intermediate–Advanced
Time	15–30 minutes
Focus	Writing/Reading creative narrative, reading out loud
Material	A recording of various types of music

Preparation

Prepare six 30-second musical excerpts. They should differ from each other in type. For example, one might be a bit of jazz followed by excerpts of muzak, rap, classical music and so on.

Procedure

1 Tell the students you are going to play them the story of somebody's holiday. But the story is told in music not words. Add that:
   - They will hear various bits of music.
   - Each bit tells the story of a different part of the holiday.

- As they listen to each excerpt, they should make notes about what the music says the person did during that part of the holiday.
- Each excerpt was, so to speak, the background music at the time.

2 Play your tape. Pause long enough between each segment for students to write their notes.
3 Ask them to change their notes into complete, first-person diary entries.
4 In pairs or groups they tell each other what they wrote, or swap and read each other's 'diaries'.

Follow on
Students prepare their own musical medleys and bring them to class for use in repeats of this activity.

Variations
- Say that each excerpt is for a completely separate holiday.
- Choose other time periods: *last weekend*, *last night*, *on my way to school* and so on.
- Form pairs. Play a medley of music relating to different holidays. After each excerpt, press the pause button and ask partners to tell each other what they do or have done on those days. Or play a medley of music relating to one particular holiday (e.g. Christmas) and ask them to write about it: What is the holiday about? What do they and other people do on that day?
- Use medleys to help students:
  - write a plot for a silent movie, where each excerpt is the background music for a different scene
  - write a fictional account of 'a day in my life', where each excerpt is the background music for a different experience
  - describe a series of real or fictional people, with each excerpt relating to a different person
  - describe a series of scenes, with each excerpt relating to a different scene

Hanna Kryszewska

6.4 Connecting the Top 50

Age	11–16
Level	Pre-intermediate–Advanced
Time	30 minutes
Focus	Writing narrative
Material	A list of the record titles in the current Top 50 (Advanced) or the Top 20 (Pre-intermediate/Intermediate)

This activity involves writing short narratives that include the titles of popular songs. It is described as it is done with students who are used to hearing English popular songs. But if your students are not used to this, see the first variation.

Preparation

1 Type out or photocopy a list of the current week's Top 50 pop songs so that each learner can have or see it. (Reduce the number to 20 or so in a pre-intermediate class.)

2 Think of an example song title story to give in Step 4 or use this one:

> Run-around-Sue told her secretary, Ricky's Girl, that in future she would have to work From 9 to 5, Eight Days a Week in Foggy London Town. Sue said I'll watch Every Move You Make. Ricky's Girl almost went Crazy thinking about all the work she would have to do. But she didn't think she could find another job. Then she had a brilliant idea. She gave Sue some coffee with sleeping pills in it and then put her on a Slow boat to China. When Sue disappeared, Ricky's Girl became the secret boss of the company. During the next few months she went from Rags to Riches.
>
> © CAMBRIDGE UNIVERSITY PRESS 2004

Procedure

1 As a warm up, ask the students which their favourite songs are at the moment and which ones they do not like, and why.

2 Distribute your handout and explain any vocabulary the students do not know.

3 Introduce or revise any particular set of connectors which you wish the students to practise.

4 Tell the students that (individually or in pairs) they are going to write a short narrative (of up to 100 words) in which they must include *at least* ten of the titles. They can, of course, use other words around the titles, but the titles must remain exactly as they are. Give a short example using a few old hit song titles.

5 Give them about 20 minutes to write their stories.

6 They share their narratives:
   - either by walking around, telling and listening
   - or in open class format (in which case, optionally, they decide which stories they like best)

Follow on

Put all the stories together in a little booklet, with the Top 50 (or 20) list at the beginning. (You can usually find a student or two willing to do this.) Photocopy and staple the booklets at school.

Variations

- If your students are familiar with mother-tongue pop songs but not English ones, then, in a previous lesson, either:
  - Form the class into groups. Assign each group a number of titles and ask them to translate as many as they can into English. Vet and collect the translations and then combine them into a list that can be used for the main activity.

  Or:
  - Make the translations yourself.

  In either case, at Step 2 give students a jumbled bilingual list of the titles and ask students to match the mother-tongue titles with the English translations.
- (In a previous lesson) Ask students to write the titles of their two favourite songs of all time on a slip of paper. Collect the slips and make a composite list of what they wrote to use as the basis for the writing activity.

Tip

Below advanced level, make the activity run more smoothly by omitting from your list any song titles that are difficult to explain or translate.

David A. Hill

6.5 Fake biographies

Age	11–13
Level	Elementary–Intermediate
Time	15–20 minutes
Focus	Writing biographies
Material	A sheet of blank A4 paper for each student

Procedure

1 Sit the students in circles of six to eight each. Give each student a sheet of paper.

2 Ask everyone to write *My name is* .... followed by their real name at the top of the sheet. They then fold what they have written back behind the sheet twice, so that it cannot be seen.

3　Collect in the sheets from Group A and swap them with those from Group B, and so on, so that everyone has someone else's paper. They *must not* look to see whose sheet they have got.

4　Tell them:

- to write *I was born in* . . . and add a place name
- that this answer and the ones to follow later can be as unusual as they like (and it is better if they are unusual!)
- to fold the sheet back, when they have finished writing, and pass it left

5　Continue dictating what they should write, and leave them to fill in the details. (After each sentence, students fold the sheet back once and pass it left.) You could dictate some or all of the following:

a	*My birthday is* . . .	(they add the date)
b	*I have* . . . *brothers and* . . . *sisters.*	(they add numbers, in words)
c	*I live in* . . .	(they add a place name)
d	*I go to school and my favourite subject is* . . .	(they add a subject)
e	*When I'm at home I like to* . . .	(they add an activity)
f	*I love music and my favourite group/ singer is* . . .	(they add a group/singer)
g	*My favourite TV programme is* . . .	(they add a programme)
h	*Last summer I went to* . . . *for my holidays.*	(they add a place)
i	*When I was there I met* . . .	(they add a person)
j	*One other thing about me is that I* . . .	(open)

6　Collect in the sheets, open them up and hand them to the person whose name is at the top. They should read them, and enjoy them!

7　They share them with their friends. There is usually much hilarity.

Follow on
Students react to the false biographies by writing correcting sentences, e.g. *I wasn't born in Africa. I was born in Italy. My favourite singer isn't Britney Spears. It's Madonna.* Or they acknowledge statements that have coincidentally turned out to be true.

David A. Hill

6.6 What a story!

Age	14 and up
Level	Pre-intermediate–Advanced
Time	5–10 minutes in one lesson, 45 minutes in the next
Focus	Telling and writing everyday stories, vocabulary relating to apparel
Material	Flashcards

Preparation

1 In the same or in an earlier lesson get your students to tell you what makes a good story: humour, varied pace of narration, suspense, surprise, and so on. Note their ideas down, for example on sheets of paper that you stick up around the room.

2 (Optional) In an earlier lesson, ask students to wear or bring in something (an item of clothing or small object) about which they can tell a story.

Procedure

1 Say that everybody carries a lot of interesting stories with them – for example, an item of clothing, an accessory, or other small personal belonging can be the centre of one.

2 Ask them to name one of the items of clothing that they can see on you. Each time they do, tell them its story: why (and where) you bought it, or who gave it to you (when and how), why you like it, when you wear it, and so on.

3 Ask your students to pair up. Then tell them they should each choose one garment, accessory or small belonging of their own and tell its story to their partner. Add that when they are in the role of listener, they should regularly request more information by asking questions such as, *Interesting! And . . .?*, *Tell me more about why . . .*

4 Working individually, students put their partner's story in writing, altering it and adding new elements in order to make it into a better story according to the criteria shown on the wall posters (see Preparation).

5 Tell everyone to exchange stories with their partner (the same person as in Step 3), read what their partner has written, and look in particular for ways in which the story has been changed from how it was told originally.

6 Onto their partner's story sheet, everyone writes a specific bit of feedback relating to 'the features of a good story', e.g. *You made the story more dramatic by . . .*

Follow on

Collect the stories, correct them and then put them up on the walls. Students mill around, reading both the stories and the feedback. Bring the class together and elicit their comments.

Hanna Kryszewska

6.7 Put yourself in the picture

Age	11 and up
Level	Upper-elementary–Advanced
Time	15–30 minutes for the writing phase
Focus	Imaginative narrative, a common way of structuring narrative, reading (or reading out loud), use of present, past and future tenses
Material	Pictures from magazines or photocopies of photographs – at least one per student, coloured markers or highlighter pens, (optional) one or more staplers

Preparation

The basic material for this activity is pictures cut from magazines or A4 photocopies of black and white photographs. Each picture should be interesting and depict a scene that (some of) your students might like to be in.

Basic options:

- Choose three or four pictures and make multiple copies of each so that students will have a (limited) choice.
- Choose a single photograph with a thematic link to something you plan to work on later (e.g. a short story) and make a class set of copies.
- If you have fewer than 25 or so students, take in a used photocopy box full of copies of various photographs, well mixed up. Everybody takes about a dozen, looks through them, chooses one and gives the others back to you.
- In an earlier lesson ask your students to bring in largish magazine pictures suitable for the activity. (This works only if they have done the activity before and know what to look for.)

Procedure

1 Distribute the pictures.
2 Say that everyone should imagine they are no longer in the classroom but in the the picture. In fact, using a coloured marker or highlighter pen,

everyone should *draw* themself *in* the picture, standing, sitting, lying, or whatever. They can be near or far, but they must be visible. Students who put themselves far into the background should make a dot where they are and draw an arrow pointing to it.

© Michael T. Murphy

3 Distribute a handout such as the one on page 135 (or display something similar on the board or OHP).

4 Explain that they are going to write down their thoughts and experiences as if they are in the picture now and have taken the time to write a postcard (or send a long voice message) to a friend back home. Add that what they write should have three parts:
   • The first and longest part is about 'now', and so here they should use present verb forms.
   • The second part is about what happened a while ago, and so they will use past forms.
   • The last part is about what comes next, and so they will mostly use future forms.
   Stress that these three parts should be in exactly this order.

5 Start them off writing, either on the back of their picture sheet or on a separate sheet. In the latter case, it is a good idea to have a stapler handy so the two sheets can eventually be attached.

6 As students finish, there are a number of options:

- In higher level classes, ask students to put their names on their story sheets and then:
  a Swap with someone else who has finished. Everyone keeps reading and swapping until the last person to finish has also had time to read at least one other student's story.
  b Go off in a corner or out into the corridor with other students who have finished and take turns showing their pictures and then reading their stories to each other.
- In lower-level classes it is often best to correct the stories before they are in some way shared in the next lesson.

Tips

ABOUT THE PICTURES

- Colour photographs tend not to copy well on the average photocopier.
- If you use more than one photograph, have a mix of ones which show people and ones which do not.
- In general, students prefer scenes with considerable distance between the foreground and the background: that is, scenes with a deep perspective.
- Poorly motivated learners can be encouraged with scenes of exotic beaches, football games, dancing, parachute jumpers or animals in them.
- Photographs from advertisements are almost never suitable.
- You may find one or two serviceable photographs in your coursebook.

ABOUT PROCEDURE

- This activity is naturally very flexible as to level. You can make it more so by stressing that not all of the questions in the first part need to be answered. Or give low- and high-proficiency students different question sheets.
- Ask early finishers to swap papers and write a couple of questions at the end of one another's stories. They then swap back and incorporate the answers to the questions into their texts, using asterisks or drawing arrows to show where any internal additions should go.

Acknowledgement

The original, basic, for-adults version of this activity is by John Morgan (Lindstromberg, ed. 1990, p. 49).

Question sheet for pre-intermediate to advanced learners

NOW

Where *exactly* are you?
What are you doing? Why?
What time of day is it?
What season is it?
What's the weather like now?
Can you hear anything? Are there any smells?
What's going on around you? Why?
How do you feel about all this?
Are there any people around? If so, what are they doing? Why?
What is the general mood? Why?

EARLIER

How did you get to this place?
Why did you come here?
What experiences or adventures did you have on the way?

SOON

What's going to happen next? Why?
What are you going to do? Why?
And then?

© CAMBRIDGE UNIVERSITY PRESS 2004

Seth Lindstromberg

6.8 Write in the shape

Age	11 and up
Level	Elementary–Advanced
Time	25–45 minutes
Focus	Writing, speaking
Material	Blank sheets of A4 paper

Procedure
See p. 10.

Variations
- Take in the papers after Step 3, and then do Step 4 in a later lesson when you have corrected the papers and handed them back.
- Ask students to fill in other outlines, e.g. of:

- a door to a house, flat or holiday home you really like(d) and remember well (*What does the door look like? Where is the house? When did/do you go there? Why do you remember this place?*)
- a key (*What is it a key to? Why is it necessary? What do you see when you open the door/lid? Where is the key now?*)
- a window you well remember looking through (*What do you see when you look out? And when you look in?*)
- a bottle (*What message would you put in it if you were on a desert island? How would you describe your life on the island so far? How did you get there? What do you want when you get back to civilisation?*)
- a favourite pair of shoes or sandals (*What do they look like? Where/When/Why did you get them? Where are they now? Where have they been? What do they make you feel like?*)
- a photo you recall (*What/Who does it show? Who took it? Where and when? What was happening just before? What happened next? If there are other people there, where are they now?*)
- the outline of a favourite singer, movie star or sportsperson (*Who is it? What does this person look like? What kinds of thing do they do that you like?*)

© CAMBRIDGE UNIVERSITY PRESS 2004

Tips
- Step 1: If after a couple of minutes a student has not thought of anything, suggest one of the following: a car, a mobile phone, a computer, a book, any musical instrument they play or an object they use in connection with a favourite sport or other pastime.

Acknowledgement
I learned about writing inside shapes from Colin Evans and Peter Grundy.

Seth Lindstromberg

Before I was 30 I never drank tea or coffee –
just water, milk, juice and, later, sometimes
beer. When I was 30 I went to Japan to
work – Tokyo, in fact. I taught English in
the morning and in the evening, but not
in the middle of the day, so I had lots of
time to kill. At first I went to the cinema
a lot, but I got tired of that. I began to read,
but I needed a place to read. I began to hang
out in coffee shops. After some time I found
I was a coffee drinker – not exactly addicted
to coffee, but nearly. Eventually I met my
now wife. She is English and loves strong
leaf tea. I developed a taste for it too and
now drink tea at least once a day. That's
why I have drawn a mug! I don't have any
special mug. At home there are several I
use. I only care about whether they are
clean and have a handle.

© Cambridge University Press 2004

6.9 Draw the text

Age	12 and up
Level	Elementary–Advanced
Time	15–25 minutes
Focus	Reading and writing spatial descriptions, speaking
Material	Copies of a text which describes a place, crayons or felt-tip pens, blank A4 paper

Preparation
1 Find and make a class set of copies of a text which describes a place.
2 Collect enough blank A4 paper and coloured markers or crayons for the whole class.

Procedure
1 Hand out copies of the text, sheets of blank paper and crayons or felt-tip pens.

2 Tell the students to read the text and draw what it describes in detail.
3 Bring the class together. Tell them to close their books.
4 Ask pairs to swap their drawings.
5 Using the drawings as prompts to memory, students each write a version of the text that is factually detailed and accurate but not necessarily in the original wording.
6 They compare what they have written with the original.

Follow on

Working individually, students each draw (for example) a plan of their kitchen. Students then swap drawings and everyone writes, or orally produces, a description from someone else's drawing.

Variations

* Allow students to work individually or in pairs, as they like.
* For a relatively small class of well-motivated learners: If you have Cuisenaire rods or small coloured building blocks, give each pair about ten and tell them to represent the text by creating some kind of arrangement. Students wander around and look at other students' creations. If puzzled by someone else's representation, students can ask them for an explanation. Students then go back to their seats and take apart their representation of the text (i.e. remove the rods or blocks), saying what each object represents as they do so.
* Use suitable song lyrics or a poem.

Hanna Kryszewska

6.10 Diary questions

Age	11–16
Level	Intermediate–Advanced
Time	30 minutes
Focus	Writing in answer to questions, speaking
Material	Diary information, as described

This collaborative writing activity, with its relevance to alibis, fits in well with a section of a coursebook to do with crime.

Preparation

1 Prepare a diary of how you spent your Saturday, Sunday or whole weekend. Give general details, but not specific ones, e.g.

Got up at 7.30. Went into town at 10.00. Home by midday. Cooked lunch for the family. Went for a drive with family. Watched film in evening.

It should be as true as possible, without you feeling you are giving away things to your students which you do not want them to know.

2   Type it out onto the top of an A4 sheet of paper.

Procedure

1   Put the class into groups of four. Tell them you want them to find out how you spent your Saturday, Sunday or weekend. Give each student a copy of the diary sheet.

2   Ask them each to read what you have written and then write one question about something they would like to know more about. Add that no one should discuss their question with the other three students in the group.

3   Each student passes their sheet to the person on their left.

4   Everyone reads the question passed to them and writes an answer *as they think you would answer it.*

5   On the same sheet, everyone writes another question (i.e. different from the first one they wrote, and the one they have just answered) which they again pass to the left.

6   Everyone again writes an answer, and so on until the papers have gone right round the group.

7   Tell your students, still in their groups, what comes next:
   • Each member of the group then reads out the four questions and answers on their sheet.
   • They discuss the likelihood of the various answers, especially whenever the same question was asked, and answered in different ways.

8   Go through your weekend with the whole class, asking groups to read out their questions and answers in chronological order. Start by saying, e.g.
   Got up at 7.30: does anyone have any questions about that time?
   Get the class to decide which answer they think is most likely for each question. You can tell them the true answer afterwards.

Follow on
Students each write a basic weekend diary, which has to be true. They form groups again, read each other's accounts and ask questions to find out the full stories.

Variations

The idea of collaborative, pass-it-round writing can be applied to other situations and to stories as well as dialogues.

- Dictate the very beginning of a story (e.g. *Dale was in a desperate situation but, as we know, she managed to escape the . . .*). Everyone completes your sentence, adds another sentence, and then passes their paper to the left (or right). Everyone then reads the story they have just received from the person on their right (or left), adds a sentence, and passes the sheet on in the same direction as before.
  (Tip: When you explain how the activity works, also say how many times the sheets will be passed. That way, students will know when to start bringing the stories towards a conclusion.)
- For dialogues, Mario Rinvolucri has proposed that the sheets of paper not travel around the group/class but that they go back and forth between pairs, like this:

Student A←—→Student B←—→Student C . . .

Dialogues can be between any two people, e.g. a prisoner and a novelist who is interviewing that prisoner during visiting hour. (Motivating background: The novelist needs material for a new novel. The prisoner wants to keep the interview going so he or she does not have to return immediately to his or her cell. Therefore, he or she wants to make her career of crime as interesting and as detailed as possible.) For example, Student A writes a question from a novelist to a prisoner and passes the sheet to B, who replies as the prisoner and then passes that sheet back to A, who adds a further line or so in the role of the novelist and so on. Meanwhile, B (as novelist) writes to C, who responds to B in the role of prisoner and so on around the class. Each student is thus engaged in two different dialogues and has a different role in each one: for instance, the role of prisoner in a dialogue with the person on their left and the role of novelist with the person on their right.

David A. Hill

Writing activities in other chapters

Short writing tasks are a feature of a number of activities throughout this book, either in the main procedure or in a follow on or variation, e.g.

1.6 (short scenario); 2.10 follow on (dialogue); 3.1 follow on (instructions); 3.3 variation (description/comparison); 3.6 follow on (description of a person); 3.8 follow on (narrative); 3.9 follow on, (narrative); 3.17 follow on (narrative); 4.3 follow on (description of a scene);

4.7 (taking dictation); 5.3 (brief narrative); 5.6 follow on (informal essay/opinion piece); 7.8 (description); 8.1 (haiku); 8.2 (limerick); 8.3 (complex sentence); 8.13 (rap lyrics)

For more on short writing activities, see Davis and Rinvolucri (1988), Brookes and Grundy (1999) and Holmes and Moulton (2001).

7 Learning and reviewing vocabulary

A key part of being a language teacher is knowing how to help students learn vocabulary both well and reasonably quickly. There are some facts about this that everyone knows: for instance, that people tend not to learn a new bit of vocabulary after encountering it just once. So, review is vitally important. What else can be said? Researchers into the matter of how vocabulary is learned and stored in memory agree about the following:

a   If you meet vocabulary in novel or emotionally coloured settings, you are more likely to notice it, pay attention to it and remember it than you otherwise might. So, we teachers should avoid always presenting and reviewing vocabulary in the same few ways.

b   You best remember vocabulary that you have not just read, but also heard; and not just heard and read, but also spoken and written. So, it is wise to adopt an integrated skills approach.

c   You are particularly likely to remember vocabulary you need in order to perform a task, especially a task which is interesting or seems intrinsically useful. Thus, the adolescent learner is especially likely to benefit from teaching which includes learning games, work with songs and plenty of communicative activities, especially centring on topics of interest to the students in the class.

d   Formation of mental links with other words is very important, especially 'collocational links' such as that between *heavy* and *rain* and 'topical links' like that between *blood* and *vampire*. (Anyone talking about vampires is likely also to talk about blood, but *blood* and *vampire* do not necessarily 'collocate', that is, occur right next to each other as do *heavy* and *rain*.) It seems likely that topic-based lessons can play a valuable role in the formation of links of both types, but we should also seek out small-scale tasks that focus sharply on the formation of mental links of one type or the other.

e   Possibly even more fundamental is the formation of mental links between vocabulary and non-verbal images – for instance, a link between the verb *spin* and a visual image of something spinning or a kinesthetic image of you yourself spinning around. And there is very strong evidence that actually acting out the meanings of vocabulary is particularly effective.

Fortunately, it is quite common for teachers to link vocabulary to pictures, realia, mime and so on. But there is doubtless more we can all do in this respect.

f Memory for a vocabulary item is enhanced if successive encounters (especially ones on different days) bring out different aspects of its meaning. For instance, if students have learned *spin* as in, *Stand up and spin around*, then it helps them also to learn that wheels can spin and that *spin* is used metaphorically (e.g. *My head is spinning*). It is especially important that our work on high-frequency words needs to take account of this.

g It is particularly easy to recall vocabulary and collocations that have been learned in meaningful contexts which are rhythmic or even melodic. Here is an additional reason for using song lyrics as well as other texts with poetic qualities.

h Having an accurate idea of *meaning* is so important for learning vocabulary that any practice which helps get vocabulary meanings across should be allowed, including – in useful ways, at appropriate times – use of the mother tongue.

i There are also some interesting findings about what makes vocabulary learning harder rather than easier. For example, Laufer (1997) observes that:

It is relatively difficult for students to learn, at the same time, vocabulary items which are:

- similar in form. So, it may be relatively hard to learn *wiggle* and *wriggle* or *put up* (*a guest*) and *put off* (*a meeting*) at the same time.
- similar in meaning. So, learning *fling* and *hurl* at the same time may be relatively hard. (This does not mean, though, that there is anything problematic in learning vocabulary in 'scenario sets', e.g. *take a bite, chew, swallow*.) It is also interesting, in this connection, that – perhaps because of underlying similarity of meaning – 'antonymic' pairs such as *borrow* and *lend* are particularly hard to learn at the same time.

As it happens, research has demonstrated that in-class vocabulary teaching can be highly effective (e.g. Hulstijn, 2001), an outcome which seems most likely if teachers take into account points (a)–(i) above. But the sheer number of words and phrases that students must learn in order to become truly proficient goes far beyond what they can possibly learn in a few years of ordinary, non-intensive language courses. To attain really good proficiency, students need to learn masses of vocabulary *outside of class*. In-class work on vocabulary, therefore, needs to go beyond the mere teaching of words and phrases. It should include, as well, work that is designed to:

- inspire students to become autonomous vocabulary learners
- educate them about effective vocabulary learning strategies

Activities completable in one or two lessons

7.1 Mime the text

Age	12 and up
Level	All
Time	15 minutes
Focus	Reading, speaking
Material	A short text (or a few very short ones), perhaps from your coursebook

Preparation

Find a suitable text or series of sentences that include fairly concrete nouns, verbs, adjectives and (perhaps) adverbs. You could lift sentences from your coursebook. For post-beginners, a text of about this long is generally suitable:

> Elephants are big and grey. African elephants have very big ears. They have long 'noses'.
> Tigers are big cats. They have long tails, stripes and sharp teeth. They eat other animals.
> Horses are big and eat grass. People ride them. They can pull heavy things.

Learners at intermediate level and above need something about as long as a medium-length paragraph or a couple of song stanzas.

Procedure

1 Make sure everyone has a copy of the text.
2 Form pairs and tell everyone to agree with their partner on a sequence of gestures that might convey the meaning of the text. For instance, to indicate *grey*, they might point to something that is grey. To indicate *Africa*, they might sketch an outline of Africa to point to. To indicate *drinks*, they can mime drinking. They may also need to agree on gestures or diagrams for particular prepositions and tenses. Encourage lower-level learners to have separate gestures for as many words as possible and more proficient learners to mime keywords only.

3 When you see that everyone is more or less finished, get the attention of the class and ask the pairs to decide who is Student A and who B.

4 Say that only Student A should look at the passage. Add that A's job is to mime each sentence in sequence (in the way just practised), pausing after each one. During A's pauses, B should say the sentence A has just mimed. Add that A should repeat prompts and correct English as necessary.

5 Partners change roles.

Follow on

- Tell the students to close their books (or turn over their papers) and either mime sentences at random, as they remember them, or mime the whole passage from beginning to end.
- If students have been working with the lyrics of a song, play the song again now. Everyone mimes the lyrics as they are sung. Different pairs will be doing different mimes, so there is high potential here for jollity.

Tip

Step 2: Allow them to *say* 'grammar words' like *a* and *the*. Or else, before the miming starts, ask the class to suggest hand signals for these and other very common unmimable grammar words.

Hanna Kryszewska

7.2 What can I see in English?

Age	12 and up
Level	Beginner
Time	10 minutes
Focus	Mainly concrete nouns and associated adjectives, raising confidence
Material	A picture in a coursebook, or handouts or an OHP transparency of a photograph

Preparation

Choose a picture in your coursebook which shows a fairly large number of people and things or prepare a class set of handouts or an OHP transparency of a suitable photograph.

Procedure

1 Students look at the picture.

2 Ask each student to think of at least three English words (not phrases or sentences) for things they can see in it.

3   Ask students, in turn, to say one of their words. Write words on the board as they are spoken. Keep going until you have a couple of dozen or more words on the board (ideally, at least one per student).
4   Divide the class into pairs.
5   Students look at the board. They take it in turns to read a word from the board. When one student in a pair calls out a word, the other points to it in the picture.

Follow on

- Bring the class together and elicit ways of combining the words on the board. So if *car* and *black* are on the board, someone might say *Black car*. (Perhaps draw arrows to connect words to words.)
- Try to elicit song and film titles or other bits of language the students may know. So if *man* is also on the board, someone might say *Men in Black*. Suggest some yourself if relatively few are forthcoming from the class.

Comment

- Even so-called beginners are almost certain to know a number of words.
- Step 2: By stipulating *at least three*, you reduce the risk that individual students will find all their words taken by someone else.

Hanna Kryszewska

7.3 How many?

Age	12 and above
Level	All
Time	10 minutes
Focus	Terms for numbers, parts of the body, clothing and accessories, (variation) relative quantifiers such as *more* and *the most*

Procedure

1   Divide your class into groups of about four or five, all, ideally, having the same number of members.
2   Ask students to count how many heads they have in their group, then noses, hands, then toes. Choose categories that will yield the same results in each group, if they are the same size.
3   Move on to categories that may yield different results for different groups, e.g. the number of pockets, trainers, glasses, rings, chains, sleeves, visible scars, shirt buttons, pencils, shoelaces, pocket flaps, logos, partings in their hair.

Variation

With learners who know *many/few, more/fewer, the most/the fewest*, ask them to discuss (for each category of thing) who has more or fewer than who, who has the most or the least, who has the highest or lowest number of each thing, who has an odd number of them and who has an even number of them and so on.

Acknowledgements

I learned the basic procedure from Bonnie Tsai at a workshop in Canterbury, England.

Hanna Kryszewska

7.4 Find the words in the picture

Age	12 and up
Level	Pre-intermediate–Advanced
Time	15–20 minutes
Focus	Review of lexical sets (mainly of concrete nouns and adjectives)
Material	Photographs, a word list, (optional) answer keys

Preparation

Collect or make the following:

- a class set of different A4 photographs that exemplify recently learned vocabulary you want to recycle (e.g. *straw hat, bushy beard, plump, wrinkles, bald*); mark each picture with a different number (*1, 2, 3 ...*)
- (optional) a set of a key, i.e. a copy of each picture with the target words written on, for example with the word *wrinkles* written on or near the face of an old person

Procedure

1   Put the pictures on the walls and number them.
2   Hand out the word lists.
3   Students walk round the class and look for the words in the pictures. Next to each word on their list, they write the number of the picture in which the word is exemplified.
4   Bring the class together and ask which pictures go with which words.

Follow on
Stick the keys on the board or wall. Students walk around and check their
work against them.

Hanna Kryszewska

7.5 Lists from pictures, pictures from lists

Age	14 and up
Level	Pre-intermediate–Advanced
Time	15–20 minutes
Focus	Adjectives and abstract nouns pertaining to faces and emotions, speaking, (variation) verbs
Material	Photographs, coloured pencils

Preparation
Collect photographs of 'emotional faces' (one per group of four), sheets of
blank paper, and coloured markers or crayons.

Procedure
1   Divide your class into groups of four or so, each group with its own
    secretary.
2   Give each group a photograph and a sheet of paper. Ask groups not to
    look at other groups' photographs.
3   Groups brainstorm adjectives and abstract nouns for the face(s) in their
    picture. For example, a picture showing three happy teenagers jumping
    with joy triggered these words: *happiness, joy, enthusiasm, friendship,
    freedom, crazy, strength, energy, jealous*. The secretary writes down all
    the words suggested.
4   Collect the photographs and ask groups to exchange lists.
5   Give each group another sheet of blank paper. (Have extra sheets ready
    in case any groups need a replacement sheet in Step 6.)
6   The groups draw a scene in which all the emotions in their new list
    would be likely. For the list in Step 3, one group of students drew a
    wedding scene. (Optionally, hand out markers and crayons.)
7   Collect the new drawings and the lists of words.
8   Display the drawings and lists (on the walls, for example) along with
    the photographs, all mixed up.
9   In pairs, students decide how the photographs, lists and drawings might
    match up. Add that different matches are possible, but each should be
    believable and justifiable.

10   Bring the class together. Discuss the various ways that pairs have matched up photographs, lists and drawings.

Variations

- At pre-intermediate level, ask for adjectives only. At intermediate level, ask for abstract nouns only.
- Have coloured paper on hand so that, in Step 6, students can choose a colour they feel is appropriate to the words on their list.
- Hand out photographs of scenes in which various actions are depicted so as to include a focus on verbs.

Tip

Find out who your best drawers are and place them in different groups so that each group not only has a secretary but also an 'artist in residence'.

Hanna Kryszewska

Note: A number of the activities that follow involve use of reproductions of photographs. A good source is www.google.com; just choose the 'images' option and do an 'advanced Google search' using keywords for the kind of scene you would like.

7.6 My schoolbag, and yours?

Age	12 and up
Level	Beginner–Advanced
Time	15 minutes
Focus	Nouns for everyday objects, (at lower levels) the grammar of countable and uncountable nouns, use of *some* versus *one* and *some* versus *any*, (at intermediate level) saying how something is useful
Material	Realia available in class

Preparation

Make sure the bag you usually bring into class is fairly well-stocked with the tools of your trade.

Procedure *(as for beginners)*

1   Open your bag. Pull out, for instance, a pencil and ask, e.g. *Have **you** got any pencils in **your** bags?*
2   Encourage your students to look into their bags and take it in turns to answer: *Yes, I've got one* or *Yes, I've got some.*
3   Form pairs and ask everyone to go through (some of) the contents of their

schoolbags item by item. For each item Student A finds, he or she should
ask their partner, B, if they have got the same thing(s). Discourage them
from looking in each other's bags. Add that if anyone needs a vocabulary
item they do not know, they can either ask you or remember the mother-
tongue word and ask later.

4 Bring the class together and ask them what words they did not know in
English. Offer dictionaries or translate the words for the students and
write them on the board.

5 Ask people to say what the most interesting things were in their partner's
bag.

Variations

• Focus on other sets of things: the contents of my fridge and yours, the
contents of my bedroom and yours, the members of my family and yours,
things in my favourite place and yours.

• Pre-intermediate and up: Ask the students to list all the usual and unusual
contents of their bags. Then ask why they bring each item. At advanced
level, follow on by focusing on one or two items and make a list of their
parts and associated vocabulary on the board, e.g. *tip, eraser, graphite,
sharp/blunt, chewed.*

Tip

Intermediate: Before beginning the variations, write a couple of 'frames' and
'sentence heads' on the board, for example *I/You need it for -ing . . . , It's
handy for when . . . , I/You . . . with it, Without it I couldn't . . .*

Hanna Kryszewska

7.7 The best . . .

Age	12 and up
Level	Post-beginner–Intermediate
Time	15 minutes
Focus	Reviewing nationality adjectives, nouns in lexical sets (especially buyable products), the grammar of plural countable nouns versus uncountable nouns, superlatives, knowledge of the world
Material	A class set of cards, each with the names of three countries on, or a set of postcards, stamps and labels from a variety of countries

Preparation

1 For each student, make a card with names of three countries written on
it. Make sure that different students mostly have different countries on

their cards. Or bring in enough postcards and labels from around the world so that each student can have three.

2   Make sure that your students know the relevant adjectives derived from names of countries (e.g. *Italy →Italian*) and the grammar of plural countable nouns (e.g. *clothes are*) and uncountable nouns (e.g. *coffee is*).

Procedure

1   Ask what kinds of things and food (for example) people can buy: *cars, computer games, chocolate, junk food, clothes* and so on. If students suggest very general things such as *software* or *vehicles*, ask them to be more specific. As students call out words, write them on the board.

2   When the board is full, give everybody a 'country card'.

3   Tell everyone they should call out plausibly true sentences of the following form:
    Nationality adjective + noun + *is/are the best!*
    A student who has *France* might use the word *clothes* (provided it is one of the words on the board) and call out *French clothes are the best!* A student with a card from Brazil might use the word *coffee* and say *Brazilian coffee is the best!*

Follow on

* Elicit sentences of the form 'Nationality adjective + noun + *isn't/aren't the best* or *may be the best* or *is/are supposed to be the best*'.
* Ask everyone to write at least two sentences. Collect and correct them.
* Invite students to add any similar comments they like, e.g. *Swiss chocolate is very expensive.*

Variations

* Step 2: Instead of cards, hand out three postcards, labels and/or stamps and say that everyone should make sure they know which country each of their postcards comes from.
* Work with the frame .... *the best in the world!* (Advise students that *the best of the world* is wrong.)
* Work with other categories of word, such as things that tourists like (e.g. *mountains, beaches, . . .*).

Hanna Kryszewska

7.8 What can you hear and smell in the picture?

Age	14 and up
Level	Pre-intermediate–Advanced
Time	30 minutes
Focus	Vocabulary relating to all the senses, speaking, writing, awareness of language and of communication skills, exam preparation
Material	A photograph in the coursebook showing a scene, e.g. a busy railway station, or photocopied photograph, one per pair

The purpose of this activity is to indicate to students how they can describe scenes more interestingly through use of vocabulary relating to senses other than sight.

Procedure

1 In pairs, students look at a particular picture in their coursebook and try to formulate a good oral description of it.

2 Bring the class together and elicit descriptions. You will probably find that their descriptions concern only what is visible.

3 On the board, draw an eye, an ear, a tongue, a hand and a nose. Explain that successful writers, from poets to people in advertising, achieve their success by referring to more than one sense.

4 Ask everyone to work in pairs again and add in what the picture suggests about sounds, smells, tastes and textures. Suppose students had earlier said:
There is a tree in the middle. A woman is sitting under it.
Say that they might expand this as follows:
There is a tree in the middle. Its trunk is smooth. In it a bird is singing. A woman is sitting under the tree. She is wearing perfume.

5 Bring the class together and ask what they have thought of. Ask also if they have learned anything about the picture through doing this exercise.

6 Ask what English expressions they would like to learn in order to be able to talk about the picture in a more effective way.

Follow on
As homework, students write fuller, multi-sensory descriptions of the same picture or of a new one.

Variation
Use photocopies of a photograph or of a reproduction of a painting. If you do this, in Step 1 students can write their notes directly onto their copies.

Then, before doing Step 2, pairs pass around their pictures so that potentially useful vocabulary is circulated around the class before they attempt their descriptions.

Tip
Step 4: Allow them to make notes in their mother tongue.

Hanna Kryszewska

Activities that can roll from lesson to lesson

7.9 Acting out prepositions

Age	7 and up
Level	All
Time	2–5 minutes
Focus	Language that can be acted out, spatial prepositions, physical action verbs, parts of the body and objects in the classroom
Material	(For one sub-activity) a class set of a handout
Function	Warm up, break, closer

Procedure

1 Now and again, in different lessons, ask students to stand. Call out a few commands such as those below and, as you do so, provide some sort of physical demonstration and ask students to follow along by acting out your commands as fully as they can. Each time, recycle expressions introduced in an earlier lesson and add a couple of new ones.

2 Write your commands on the board for students to copy down.

Follow on
In later lessons:
- Show/Explain key meaning relations such as the following:
    - *Near* includes *beside, just above/over/under/below/in front of/behind*.
    - *By* is similar to *near* except that it does not usually include *just above/under*.
    - *Below* is more specific than *under*. X *is below* Y means X *is not touching* Y.
    - *Underneath* is more specific than *under*. *Underneath* means *really under, probably hidden*.
    - *Behind* is not quite the same as *on the other side of*. *Behind* means *just on the other side of something and (potentially) hidden by it*.

- Call two or three students to the front of the class and ask them to call out commands which the other students have to perform.
- Do 'LEGO® constructions' (3.1) and 'Picture dictation – a basic version' (4.3).

Variations

- Younger learners may find learning more interesting if target vocabulary generally (not just prepositions) is used in the context of a game such as 'Simon says' for which the key rule is that students should only act out a command if it is in the form *Simon says, . . .* , e.g. *Simon says, 'Put your hand on your head'*. If you give the bare command, *Put your hand on your head*, they should do nothing. The object of the game, from your students' point of view, is not to let you trick them into performing bare commands. There is a forfeit each time someone is tricked, e.g. you erase one letter from a phrase on the board and when the phrase is all gone the game is over. Or do the opposite and build a word letter by letter, finishing the game when the word is complete. Or rub out elements of a drawing one by one. Or do the opposite and build up a drawing.
- In 'Do as I say, (not as I do)', a variation of 'Simon says', you give the command and, as you do so, either act out the corresponding action or try to trick students by acting out a *different* action from what you said so that students have to listen carefully.

Acknowledgement

This way of teaching prepositions and associated vocabulary is related to Total Physical Response. (See www.tpr-world.com.) For more on the meanings of prepositions see Lindstromberg (1997).

Example commands

- *Hands up, hands down, Stand up, sit down.*
- *Lean/Step left/right/back/forward.*
- *Lean on your desk.*
- *Arms up/down.*
        out (in front of you) / (to the sides).
        back.
        at your sides.
- *Press your arms against your sides.*
- *Feet together/apart.*
- *One hand in front of your face.*
        on your head.
        over/above your head.
        behind your head.
        under your chin.
- *Make an 'O' with a thumb and a finger. Look through it.*
- *Hold a hand in front of your face. Fingers together/Fingers apart. Put your nose between two fingers.*
- *Touch a shoulder with a finger. Run your finger along your arm to your wrist. Now back again.*
- *Touch your nose. Move your finger from your nose to the top of your head.*
- *Imagine two pencils or pens. Lay one on your table. Lay the other one beside/alongside it, like this. (Indicate the position of the pencils with your fingers.)*
- *Imagine two coins. Put one on your table. Put the other one beside it.*
- *Put a book in the middle of your desk. Now in a corner. In the middle again. Now near you. Turn it around. Turn it over. Turn it over and over. Now around and around. Open it. Put a pencil in it. Close it. Take the pencil out. Put the book near you again. Put the pencil beside/on/under/in front of it. Now put it on the other side of the book from you. Stand the book up. Put the pencil behind it so you can't see it. Now put the book over it. Where is it?*
- *Take a sheet of paper. Pick up a pencil. Hold it and get ready to draw. Put the tip in the lower left corner. Draw a line along the bottom edge. Look at the left edge. Find the middle. Put your pencil tip there. Draw a line straight across the paper.*
- *Draw a square. Draw another square inside it. The one inside should not touch the other one!*
- *Draw a glass full of juice. Where is the juice? (Note: Inside is not a natural answer because we mainly use inside with objects, not substances.)*

Seth Lindstromberg

7.10 **Memory poster circles**

Age	11 and up
Level	All
Time	15–25 minutes for the main procedure, less when reviewing in later lessons
Focus	Teaching and consolidating the memory of action verbs, (follow on) methods usable in independent word study, (variation) vocabulary in general
Material	Blank sheets of paper, felt-tip pens

The activity works most straightforwardly in classes of 12–30 students, with eight as an absolute minimum.

Preparation

Prepare a list of words or very short phrases that you wish to teach or review. If you have 8–15 students, plan to assign one to each student. If you have 16–30, form pairs and assign one item to each pair. In general, your aim should be to make a list such that everyone knows some of the words but nobody knows them all, and nobody already knew the particular item that you assign them.

Procedure (for a class of 16–30)

THE FOUNDATION

1   Ask everyone to stand. Call out the vocabulary items you have chosen one by one and ask students to follow you in enacting/miming each item.
2   Invite anyone to enact or mime any of the movements they can remember. Add that when anyone performs one of the actions, they or anyone else who remembers the verb can say it. (You say it if no one else can.) As actions are remembered, write the corresponding verbs on the board.
3   Add onto the board any verbs that no one remembered and elicit or perform the action for each one.
4   Ask students to pair up but try not to put two very low-proficient students together.
5   Assign each pair a different verb, check that they know what it means, and ask them to produce a poster on a blank sheet of paper as follows:
   • In the largest letters possible they write the initial and maybe also final consonant(s). The middle of the verb (e.g. the vowel) is represented by a dash. So, *sway* becomes *SW–* or *SW–Y, lean*

becomes *L–––* or *L–N* and so on. Phrases may be written in a number of ways, e.g. *take a bite* can be *t–ke a b–* or t– *a b–*).

- In one corner of the poster, they make a sketch that in some way suggests the meaning of the verb. For *sway*, this might be a standing stick figure with arrows which suggest side-to-side movement; for *take a bite*, an apple with a bite missing.

6   All the pairs stand against the walls and hold up their posters.

7   Right around the circle, each pair says their word or phrase and enacts its meaning.

CONSOLIDATION

8   Call on one pair. As a team, the two partners point to several of the other posters and perform the appropriate movements. Any pair whose verb or phrase is acted out must call it out clearly.

9   Repeat with a couple more pairs.

10   Ask everyone, with their partner, to look at all the posters (which are still being held up) and try to remember both the movement and word(s) for each.

11   Ask pairs to form a giant horseshoe. Position those who you suspect have the best memories for vocabulary at one end and those who you think do not, at the other.

12   Start with the least confident pair. They say their own verb or phrase. The next pair says the first pair's word(s) and their own. And so on.

13   (Optional) Students mingle, show each other their posters, and explain their sketches to each other.

14   Either collect the posters or ask students to stick them on the walls around the room.

Follow on

- In the same or in a later lesson, ask the pairs to form a horseshoe (or circle) in a different order and fold their posters so that only the initial consonant is visible. All at the same time, the members of each pair look at all the other posters and try to remember and enact each verb, pointing to the relevant poster each time.
- In later lessons, perhaps just as class begins or just before it ends, call a couple of students to the front of the class. Point to different posters (if they are on the walls) or display them by hand and elicit the words from the class. The students at the front of the class carry out the appropriate movements.

- When one set of verbs has been fairly well learned, introduce more in the same way. Eventually, there may be a few dozen posters on the walls. Take down posters for items that have been learned and keep them in a box for later review (i.e. use them as flashcards).
- Test students on their recollection of verbs and verb phrases by asking students to write out the numbers *1* to *20* (for example). Then, number by number, perform the actions for the expressions you want to test them on. For example, call out *Number 1* and bend over. Students should write *bend over* next to number 1, and so on. (I generally ask students to work in pairs, i.e. with one quiz sheet between them.)

Variation

You can also work with non-enactable vocabulary that your class have already learned in some conventional way, e.g. while working through a reading passage. (a) Ask individuals or pairs each to choose a word or short phrase (e.g. from the text) that they want to remember. (b) Ask them to make posters as in Step 5 above. (c) Use the posters as in Steps 6–14, but (probably) without any enactment.

Example action expressions and approximate levels

Beginner/Elementary: *stand, sit, pick up, put down, turn around, look up/down, step forward/back/left/right, push, pull, jump, throw, catch, drink, eat, take off (a hat), put on (a hat), play the piano/a guitar, read, write, walk, run, sleep, cry, laugh*

Pre-intermediate: *lean right/left/back, bite, take a bite, chew, swallow, bend over, wave, nod, shake, stare, fold, tear, drop, blow, sneeze, cough, blow your nose, shout, breathe in/out, point at*

Intermediate: *sway, swing, spin (around), beat (your chest), stretch, yawn, scratch, rub, glance, dip, stir, sip, wrap, tie a knot, twist, pop, do up/undo (your shoelaces)*

Upper-intermediate: *toss (a ball), chuck (it in the bin), stroke, shove, gulp, gobble, hiccup, rip, wink, blink, screw up/flatten out (a sheet of paper), slap, punch, chop, giggle, snap, click, pose (for a photograph), inhale/exhale, cuddle (a baby)*

Advanced: *beckon, slump, nudge, poke, fling, stagger, limp, gasp, glare, duck, dodge, snort, flap (your arms), wiggle (a finger), wriggle, jab, cast (a net), hurl (a boulder), fidget, flinch, flex (your muscles), squeak*

Tip

Step 5: Circulate and make sure the pairs can each explain the connection between their sketch and their verb.

Seth Lindstromberg

7.11 Physical action vocabulary and metaphor

Age	13 and up
Level	Intermediate–Advanced
Time	10–15 minutes for the main procedure
Focus	Physical action vocabulary, awareness of metaphor
Material	(Optional) an OHP transparency and OHP

Preparation

1 Choose a set of previously learned verbs and new metaphorical expressions to work with: 8 to 12 is usually about right. (See p. 158 for a list of verbs.) Examples of their metaphorical usage (either as verbs or as derived nouns or adjectives) can be found in a good dictionary, e.g. *a <u>sway</u>able child, a <u>snap</u> decision, <u>pop</u> the question, <u>nudge</u> someone into action, <u>shaken</u> by the news, my head is <u>spinning</u>, <u>stretch</u> the truth, a <u>dip</u> in confidence, a mood <u>swing</u>.*

2 Prepare a jumbled (but numbered) list of expressions in some of which the action verbs (or derived nouns/adjectives) you have chosen are used literally and in others of which the vocabulary is used metaphorically.

3 For the second follow on, prepare a set of newspaper headlines in which known action vocabulary is used metaphorically.

Procedure

1 Display your list of expressions on the board (or via OHP).

2 Taking the expressions one by one, ask which are literal and which metaphorical and for the latter elicit guesses about the connection between the movement they learned for the verb and the new usage.

3 Rub the list off the board and then ask students to tell the expressions back to you while someone writes them on the board again.

Follow on
Hand out newspaper headlines which include learned action verbs used metaphorically (e.g. *Bright future beckons*, *Ten caught in police swoop*). Elicit guesses about their meanings.

Seth Lindstromberg

Vocabulary elsewhere in this book
Most of the activities in this book involve some learning or reviewing of vocabulary. See, in particular, 'Topics' and 'Vocabulary' in the Index.

8 Literature

Why do foreign literature with adolescents at all?

- Largely, literature is about ways of being human, and so embraces questions such as these:

  Why do people do the things they do? How do other people think and feel? What is important? How should we live? What happens when we do not live the way we should? What is love? How should we think of ourselves? How should we think of death? What is the past and what does it mean? What will the future bring? What is *out* there?

  An interest in such matters may never be more vivid in us than when we are young. And literature in another language may provide as many avenues to consideration of such existential matters as may literature in one's mother tongue.

- A considerable amount of any language will remain incomprehensible to people who lack knowledge of its cultural bases. This is most obviously true of the registers of language that one needs to forge a way through university and flourish (or at least cope) in the haunts of the well-educated.

  Literature is a major element of culture. Furthermore, it is a window on all the other elements: on religion, on beliefs generally, on shared views on the past, on folklore, on language itself.

- It is good to expose students to a language as it is used day in and day out by people in all walks of life who have not the time to labour over what they write and say. But it is good too that students should once in a while get to grips with language as set down with thought, care and passion by someone who has a cultivated talent for wording. Great turns of phrase stick in our minds, and research into memory suggests that rhythm, rhyme, alliteration, allegory and certain other expressive devices may never have a firmer grip on us than when we are young. Doing foreign literature may therefore swell learners' ability to express themselves with clarity and effect.

- Doubts still? Consider that nothing is loved by everyone – not even the lessons we normally teach. Also, it *is* a possibility that more students have a liking for literature, or may come to have one, than we might at first suspect.

Assuming that you decide to look further below, in this chapter you will find several 'old reliables', activities which no collection should be without because they work so well when used with the right sort of text. There are as well activities which you may find fairly new. Most of the activities involve work with given literary texts, but some (the first three) involve learning about aspects of literary language through writing, not just through reading or listening.

Note: At such sites as www.poets.org/poems you can find hundreds of poems, many that are now in the public domain. Additionally, you can often find the complete text of an older poem or short story simply by going to a search engine and typing in the author's name and/or title.

Writing poetic texts: learning about basic features of poetic writing

8.1 Writing haikus

Age	13 and up
Level	Upper-elementary–Advanced
Time	25 minutes
Focus	Vocabulary (especially nouns for feelings and time expressions), syllabification, writing, the concept of poetic structure
Material	One slip of paper for each student

Procedure
1 Give each student a slip of paper.
2 Ask them to write an abstract noun for an emotion or attitude on one side of the piece of paper. Give a couple of examples, such as *envy*, *trust*, *happiness*.
3 Ask them to write a time of day or night on the other side of the paper: *dawn* or *half past three*, for instance.
4 Collect all the slips of paper and shuffle them up.
5 Students each pick a slip. (They return it if it is one that they themselves wrote.)
6 Check your students know what a syllable is.
7 Write the numbers 5, 7, 5 on the board and tell everyone:
   • You would like them to write three lines of text that tell a story (or describe a picture).

- *But*, the first line should have only five syllables in it, the second exactly seven, and the third five.
- They should combine the two expressions on their slip as follows: noun + time. For example, *love at noon*.
- They should use this combination somewhere in their haiku.

Follow on

- Students share their texts with each other in some manner, e.g. they read them out to each other in groups.
- If they did not know before, tell them that what they have written are haikus.
- If you have access to the Internet, then go to a search engine such as www.google.com and type in *haikus*. You will find lots of sites, some with student-made haikus on them. Your students can read these and/or post up their own creations.

Variation

Use other kinds of phrases, e.g.

- emotion + place/occasion as in *disappointment in London* or *hope at breakfast*
- sound + place as in *laughter in the kitchen* or *a roar in the garden*

Tips

- Step 2: Encourage use of bilingual dictionaries.
- See Holmes and Moulton (2001) for more on getting students to write haikus and other kinds of short poem.

Acknowledgement

I learned this activity from Christoph Kühne who learned it on a workshop in Switzerland.

Example haikus

Envy at sunset.	There was no honey	(5)
It will soon be night. I would	or toast – disappointment at	(7)
like to be an owl.	eight in the morning.	(5)

© CAMBRIDGE UNIVERSITY PRESS 2004

Tessa Woodward

8.2 Writing limericks

Age	13–16
Level	Intermediate–Advanced
Time	45 minutes
Focus	Writing, reading out loud, rhythm and rhyme, the concept of poetic structure
Material	Examples of limericks

Preparation

On a handout or on the board or OHP, write a couple of standard limericks. These are two which I often use:

There was an old man of Devizes	There was a young man from Bengal,
Whose ears were of different sizes.	Who went to a fancy-dress ball.
The one that was small	He went, just for fun,
Was of no use at all	Dressed up as a bun,
But the other won several prizes.	And a dog ate him up in the hall.

Procedure

1 Elicit from or explain to your students that:
   - the limerick is a comical five-line poem in which lines A, B and E rhyme
   - each of these lines has three stresses
   - lines C and D also rhyme (usually)
   - each of these lines has two stresses
2 Read the limericks to them, and beat the time as you do.
3 Get them to read them with you and beat the time too. In this way they will get the feel of the limericks.
4 Ask them to think of some single-syllable English names (e.g. *Paul, Anne, Mike, Jane, Liz, Steve, Pete*). As they shout these out, list them on the board. If they do not give you *Sue*, elicit it by asking, *What is the short form of* Susan?
5 Elicit words which rhyme with *Sue* and write them on the board. (The basic core of common words is: *blew, blue, chew, clue, crew, do, few, flew, 'flu, glue, grew, knew, moo, new, ooh, queue, shoe, threw, through, to, too, true, two, view, who, you, zoo*. They may need all these, so give them ones you cannot elicit. More advanced words are: *brew, cue, dew, due, ewe, flue, gnu, hue, mew, pew, screw, shoo, skew, slew, stew, sue, yew*.)

6   Write the following table up on the board or OHP:

	Article	Adjective (1 syllable)	Person (2 syllables)	Verb	Name (1 syllable)
There was	a/an			called named	Sue

7   Elicit –
   • single-syllable adjectives such as *old, young, fat, thin, big, small, tall, short, bad, good, red, sad, cold, nice*
   • two-syllable words for a person, e.g. *lady, woman, person, student, teacher, sister, brother, cousin, father, mother, doctor, tailor, singer, writer*
   And list them under the columns in the grid.
8   Students work in pairs (or alone, if they prefer) and write the first line of their limerick by choosing words to fit in the pattern shown by the grid, e.g. *There was a fat doctor called Sue.*
9   They write a second line which must end with one of the rhyming words you wrote up earlier (Step 5). If anyone seems to be finding this difficult, suggest that '*Who* + past simple verb' is a good start to the second line, e.g. *There was a fat doctor called Sue / Who went* . . . Circulate, helping them with the stress and rhythm.
10 Lines C and D must be in the correct rhythm, but do not absolutely need to rhyme. For example, the following – while not ideal – is acceptable:

   *There **was** a fat **doct**or called **Sue** / Who **went** to **vis**it the **zoo**. / As **soon** as she **got** there / The **el**ephant **said** /* . . . [Stresses: 3, 3, 2, 2]

11 Students write the final line, which must rhyme with the first two, again using one of the rhyming words written up in Step 5, e.g. *To **see** me, just **wait** in the **queue**.*
12 Students read their limericks out loud to the class, or to each other in groups.

Follow on
   • Put the limericks together as a collection. (You can usually find a student who has a computer and is prepared to type them up for you.)
   • Students write other limericks using the same formula.
   • Give them some other examples to read.

David A. Hill

8.3 Word association poems

Age 14 and up
Level Intermediate–Upper-intermediate
Time 15–20 minutes
Focus Writing complex sentences, reading aloud, blank verse (i.e. awareness of the potential for poetic effects in what is basically prose)

Procedure

1 Ask everyone to think of a noun they like in English, to write it on a sheet of paper and circle it.
2 Everyone passes their sheet with the word on it to another student.
3 Ask everyone to:
   • write five or six new words that come to them by free association when they think of the word in the circle
   • arrange these words as shown in the figure below
   Add that:
   • any kind of plausible association is acccptable
   • the new words do not have to be nouns
4 Everyone passes their paper to a different student.
5 Explain that everyone should write *one* sentence about the encircled noun which uses all the associated words (but not the encircled noun itself).

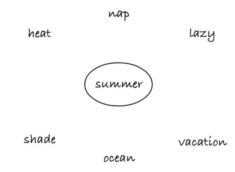

For example:

On <u>vacation</u> by the <u>ocean</u> I like to take a <u>lazy</u> <u>nap</u> during the <u>heat</u> of the day in the <u>shade</u>.

6 Ask students to divide their sentence into sense groups and put each one on a different line so that the sentence looks like a poem, like this:

On vacation
by the ocean
I like
to take a lazy nap
during the heat of the day
in the shade.

7   Students read their poems to each other. (Stress that they should pause noticeably at the end of each line.)

Follow on
Students swap texts and read them out again (so that everyone hears their own text read to them).

Comment
Students may not realise they have written something with poetic qualities until, as in the last step, they read their work out to someone else, or hear it read back to them. This activity is, therefore, a kind of 'back door' to the production and appreciation of literary texts. Much depends, however, on the manner of reading and so it may be prudent to do 'Reading aloud' (5.7) shortly before doing this.

Bonnie Tsai

First encounters with poetic texts: preparing for reception, hearing/reading

8.4 From words to predictions

Age	11 and up
Level	Pre-intermediate–Advanced
Time	15–20 minutes
Focus	Speaking, listening, reading
Material	A class set of copies of a poem or song lyric, (variation) short story

Preparation
1   Find a short literary text (e.g. poem or song lyric) that tells or implies a scenario.
2   Make a list of *all* the nouns in the text.

Procedure
1   Write the nouns on the board in the order they occur in the text.
2   Ask students each to choose the three which they think are the most positive, for any reason.

3 Form groups of four and ask students to say briefly what words they have chosen and why.

4 Ask each group to come up with at least two quite different answers to the following questions:

Thinking only of the words chosen by members of your group, what could a poem (song lyric) that contains those words be about? That is:

a Who might be speaking (or singing)?

b Speaking (or singing) to whom?

c Where and when?

d Suppose there is a story in the poem (or song). What is its beginning and what is its end?

e What happened before the story began?

f Suppose there is a problem in the poem (or song). What is it?

© CAMBRIDGE UNIVERSITY PRESS 2004

---

5 Ask the groups to divide in half. Ask each half to join a half from another group.

6 Ask everyone to:
   • tell their new partners what scenarios their original group thought of
   • choose the best scenario from all the ones they have talked about

7 Bring the class together and ask what the best scenarios were.

8 Ask students to listen especially for similarities to any of the scenarios they have heard and then read out the poem (or play the song) to them.

9 Ask students for comment first on similarities and then on anything else they heard.

10 Give them the poem or lyrics to read.

Variations

There are many variations on the basic idea, for example:

At Step 4:
• Write up some of the verbs that are in the text.
• Ask students to work individually and group the words into a small number of sets and give each set a heading. Then ask them each to choose a couple of words from each of their sets and think of a scenario that includes them. (Prompt them with the questions from Step 4.) In pairs or

threes, students explain their classifications and tell their scenarios.
Continue with Step 6.

- Preview a short story by presenting a list of about a dozen key nouns, plus
  the name (and a brief description) of each of the main characters.
  Students compose scenarios by taking all the words and names into
  account.

Comment
After working with relevant vocabulary, students are better equipped than
otherwise they might be to understand the text when they hear or read it the
first time.

Having invested time and thought in making predictions, students
are especially likely to pay attention to the text when they do finally
encounter it.

Seth Lindstromberg

8.5 Find the poem

Age	11 and up
Level	Pre-intermediate–Advanced
Time	5–10 minutes
Focus	Listening, reading
Material	A class set of a handout (see Preparation)

Preparation
1 Find a four- to eight-line poem (or an equivalent passage of a long poem)
  whose individual lines are fairly short.
2 Type up the poem and then add sentences, words and phrases around and
  within it as shown in the examples on pp. 170–171.

Procedure
1 Read out the poem (or play a recording), leave a period of ten seconds or
  so of silence, and then read the poem again.
2 Distribute the handouts and ask students to underline or highlight *only*
  the words that they remember you saying. Deal with any questions about
  vocabulary.
3 Put students in groups of four or so and ask them to take turns reading
  out to each other what they have underlined.
4 Read the poem a final time.

5   Elicit various versions of the poem from the groups.
6   Write the poem on the board.

Follow on
Proceed to work on a song that is about the same topic as the poem.

Variation
Use short texts of other sorts, e.g. stanzas of songs, a bit of dialogue from a play, the opening of a short story or novel, news-in-brief articles.

Comment
One aim is to help students notice how the poem is put together at a fairly basic level: what are its words and where are they? A subsidiary aim is to exemplify how the expressive power of writing may be enhanced through the judicious removal of the superfluous.

PRE-INTERMEDIATE

Nursery rhyme

Original

Star light!
Star bright!
First star I see tonight.
I wish I may, I wish I might,
Have the wish I wish tonight.

Padded out version

You are a star so light!
You are a star so bright!
Because you are the first star that I see tonight,
I wish I may, I wish I might,
Have the wish I wish on you tonight.

INTERMEDIATE

From 'Sing-Song' (Christina Rossetti, on the Internet)

Original

O Lady Moon, your horns point toward the east;
Shine, be increased:
O Lady Moon, your horns point toward the west;
Wane, be at rest.

Padded out version

I see, O Lady Moon, how your two horns point toward the east;
So shine, this means you will be increased:
Now it's two weeks later and, O Lady Moon, your horns both point toward the west;
This means you will wane, and be at rest.

UPPER-INTERMEDIATE

'Love without hope' by Robert Graves (from *Collected Poems*. 1975.
A. P. Watt)

Original

Love without hope, as when the young bird-catcher
Swept off his tall hat to the Squire's own daughter,
So let the imprisoned larks escape and fly
Singing about her head, as she rode by.

Padded out version

This is about love without hope, as when, for example, the young bird-catcher
Swept off his tall hat to the Squire's own daughter when he saw her coming on her
    horse,
And so let the imprisoned larks, which he had been keeping under his hat, escape
    and fly up
Singing about her head, as she rode by looking at him with great surprise.

Seth Lindstromberg

8.6 Gradual reveal

Age	11 and up
Level	Pre-intermediate–Advanced
Time	30–45 minutes
Focus	Reading and discussing a poem, (follow on) re-writing a poem as prose
Material	A poem or very short story that is (ideally) rich in narrative, (optional) the poem on OHP transparency, OHP

If the poem you are using has a surprise ending, 'Gradual reveal' is a particularly good way of making sure that it has the greatest possible effect on your class.

Preparation

If possible, copy the poem onto an OHP transparency so that you can easily reveal the poem section-by-section. More laborious alternatives are to photocopy the sections on separate sheets of paper or to write up on the board or dictate each section.

Procedure

1 Reveal the title and ask your students what they think the poem is going to be about.
2 Reveal sections of the poem one by one, i.e. individual lines, or verses, or groups of verses. (How much you reveal at once depends on the poem.) With each reveal, pose questions about the text and invite predictions about what will come next.

Follow on

For homework, the students write the story in prose.

EXAMPLE (INTERMEDIATE–ADVANCED)

The slashes show feasible break points.

A Visit to the Asylum (Edna St Vincent Millay)

Once from a big, big building,
When I was small, small,
The queer folk in the windows
Would / smile at me and call.

And in the hard wee gardens
Such pleasant men would hoe:
"Sir, may we touch the little girl's hair!"
It / was so red, you know.

They cut me colored asters
With shears so sharp and neat,
They brought me grapes and plums and pears
And / pretty cakes to eat.

And out of all the windows,
No matter where we went,
The merriest eyes would follow me
And / make me compliment.

There were a thousand windows,
All latticed up and down.
And up to all the windows,
When / we went back to town,

The queer folk put their faces,
As gentle as could be;
"Come again, little girl!" they called, and
I / called back, "You come see me!"

Other usable poems
Ages 12 and up:

- Intermediate–Advanced: 'It was long ago' by Eleanor Farjeon (p. 188)
- Upper-intermediate–Advanced: 'The Shooting of Dan McGrew' and 'The Cremation of Sam McGee' by Robert Service (both on the Internet)

Ages 13 and up:

- Upper-intermediate–Advanced: 'The Raven' by Edgar Allan Poe (on the Internet)

Ages 15 and up:

- Upper-intermediate–Advanced: 'The Last Dessert' by Glynn Maxwell (1990, *The Tale of the Mayor's Son*, Bloodaxe Books) Reveal verses in six goes: 1–3, 4, 5–6, 7–8, 9, 10–13; 'I remember, I remember' by Thomas Hood (on the Internet)

David A. Hill

Learning a poem really well: reading out loud and/or memorising

8.7 Starting and ending with dashes

Age	7 and up
Level	Any
Time	10–15 minutes
Focus	Enjoying a short poem, pronunciation, (follow on) memorising a poem

Procedure

GUESSING THE POEM

1 Write on the board a dash for each word of the first line of the poem you have selected. Thus, if the first line of the poem is *Do not go quietly*, you write on the board: _ _ _ _ . Do the same for the second and all the remaining lines of the poem.
2 Line by line, elicit the words of the poem from your students dash by dash using any kind of hint you can think of (e.g. mime, first letter hints, antonyms, fingers held up to indicate the number of letters). Write each word on top of its line on the board.

3 Say the completed poem out loud and ask the class to tell you which words or syllables you stressed and which words rhyme.

4 Ask the students to say the poem after you as you read it out again.

5 Put students into A/B pairs and ask them to read the poem off the board to each other as follows: A reads the first line, B the second and A the third and so on until they finish. Then they swap and B reads the first line and A the second and so on.

6 Ask students to write it down in their notebooks.

MEMORISING THE POEM

7 Lead students in reciting the poem.

8 When you are sure all can read the poem reasonably well, go to the board and erase words slowly one at a time in different lines, leaving the dashes. Students will often start to laugh or protest at this point but if you do not do it too fast, they will see that the challenge is to keep 'reading' the poem off the board even when words have been rubbed off and are not there. The dashes will of course remind them where words were.

9 Before too long students will be helping each other to read a poem off the board using only the dashes.

10 Bring the class together and all together recite the poem from memory.

Follow on

Once or twice in later lessons ask students to form pairs and try to recall the poem without looking in their notebooks. On the board, write prompts as necessary (e.g. every second rhyming word). Then bring the class together for a quick group recital.

Tip

Step 1: Discourage students from writing any part of the poem down until Step 6.

Comment

Good sources of short poems are Benson, et al. (1999) and Williams (1976).

Tessa Woodward

8.8 Picture poem

Age	5 and up
Level	Any, but especially Post-beginner–Intermediate
Time	About 20 minutes depending on the length of the poem
Focus	Enjoying, listening to, reciting and memorising a poem, pronunciation
Material	A few sets of pictures which you draw or find, (first variation) just one set of pictures

Preparation

1   Select a short poem that mentions physical actions.
2   Draw pictures that match the lines of the poem (or find pictures in magazines, cut them out and photocopy them). Thus, if your first line is *Cats sleep on sofas*, find or draw a simple picture of a cat asleep on a sofa. If your second line is *Cats eat mice*, find or draw a picture of a cat eating a mouse. You need at least one picture for each line and one set of pictures for each group of four to six students.

Procedure

1   Put the class into groups and give each group a jumbled set of pictures.
2   Tell your class that you will read a poem out loud and that they have to listen and, in their groups, move the pictures into the order in which the actions are mentioned in the poem.
3   Read or say the poem slowly out loud, watching that the students start moving the pictures into order. You may have to repeat the poem two or three times for students to check that they have got the order right.
4   Say the first line. Have them (1) say it after you and (2) point at the correct picture.
5   Repeat this with the second line of the poem. Then loop back: that is, ask students to point at the first picture and say the first line and then point at the second picture while saying the second line. Continue in this way (i.e. advance one line, then review the whole poem up there, advance another line and so on).
6   Divide the class in half. Have the left half say the odd lines and the right half say the even ones.
7   Divide the class into pairs and have them say alternate lines each. Encourage them to use the pictures to prompt their memories.
8   Ask everyone to write the poem in their notebooks.

Follow on
In later lessons, hand out the pictures again. Students put them in order and
try to recite the poem from memory.

Variations
- Step 1: Make just one set of pictures and display them where everyone
  can see them. Call one or two students up and ask them to order the
  pictures as you say the poem.
- Step 6: If the poem is suitable, ask everyone to mime the actions that are
  mentioned.
- The technique of asking students to order pictures can be applied to
  work with many longer poems that you do not intend students to
  memorise.

Tip
Step 4: Tell students not to write the poem down until you ask them to (Step
8).

EXAMPLE POEMS/RHYMES

Post-beginner–Pre-intermediate: 'There are Big Waves' (Eleanor Farjeon).
Capitals added to show rhythm.

There are BIG waves and LIttle waves,
GREEN waves and BLUE,
WAVES you can JUMP over,
WAVES you dive THROUGH.

WAVES that rise UP like a
GREAT water WALL,
WAVES that swell SOftly and
DON'T break at ALL.

WAVES that can WHIsper,
WAVES that can ROAR,
TIny waves that RUN at you,
RUnning on the SHORE.

Elementary–Advanced: 'Cats sleep anywhere' (Eleanor Farjeon).

Cats sleep
Anywhere,
Any table,
Any chair,
Top of piano,
Window-ledge,
In the middle,
On the edge,
Open drawer,
Empty shoe,
Anybody's
Lap will do,
Fitted in a
Cardboard box,
In the cupboard
With your frocks –
Anywhere!
They don't care!
Cats sleep
Anywhere.

Tessa Woodward

8.9 Technicolour reading: recital in voice groups

Age	14 and up
Level	Intermediate–Advanced
Time	20 minutes
Focus	Reading and understanding a poem, awareness of key factors in successful choral recitation, teamwork
Material	Any kind of poem (to be photocopied unless fairly short)

Preparation

1 Select a poem that you would like to share with your students: ideally, it should be at least ten lines long, divisible into sense chunks of some kind, e.g. episodes, sections on different topics, things seen or thought at different times, thoughts or viewpoints of different people, questions and answers.

2   If it is too long to write on the board, make copies of it.

3   You will assign different parts of the poem to groups of students with different qualities of voice, so think now about which parts should be read by students with low voices, which by students with high voices and so on. (See Steps 4–6.)

Procedure

1   Hand out copies of the poem and make sure students understand it.

2   Check that they are fairly clear about how to read it with acceptable pronunciation and rhythm.

3   Lead the whole class in reading the poem out loud until they sound good.

4   Explain that they all have very nice voices, some light and some dark, some slower, some faster and that you are all going to listen to everyone read a little or speak a little so you can put them into voice groups.

5   Ask them each to speak or read aloud in any language and then make groups of students who have, for example:
   • darker, lower or slower voices
   • lighter, higher or faster voices
   • particularly strong, dramatic voices

6   Say which sense chunks of the poem should be said by which voice groups.

7   Ask the different voice groups to highlight or underline on their copies the parts they are going to say.

8   Have a couple of runs through with the whole class until the group can recite the poem smoothly and dramatically with the different voice groups saying their parts.

Follow on
• Perform the reading in front of another class, parents or other teachers.
• In later lessons, form groups of students with different voice qualities. In their groups, students decide themselves how to divide up a poem and who is going to read which part(s). Groups can read out different poems or they can all read out the same poem (but probably in different ways).

Variations
- Between Steps 7 and 8, allow groups to rehearse their parts.
- Readings can be prepared too using other effects such as: varied volume, pitch, speed; choral/single voices; pauses; repeats; sound effects (e.g. rhythm marked by clicks, claps or slaps; background vocal hums or hisses; wind-like moans; footsteps).

Tip
Step 4: Involve students as much as possible in decisions about which voice groups they should each go in and make sure you compliment all students and all voice groups for the particular quality of voice they have.

Comment
This activity helps students feel what it is like to work as a group towards a performance. They also learn more about the timbre of their own voices.

Tessa Woodward

Exploring the meanings of literary texts: reading, thinking, discussing

8.10 Poem picture metaphor

Age	11 and up
Level	Upper-elementary–Advanced
Time	10–25 minutes
Focus	Reading, noticing and discussing similarities
Material	A poem (optionally, a class set) and a picture that you have chosen to go with it (see Preparation and Variations for different possibilities)

This is a good follow on from any activity which has brought students to the point where they already understand a poem fairly well, e.g. 'From words to predictions' (8.4), 'Find the poem' (8.5) and 'Gradual reveal' (8.6).

Preparation
1   Choose a poem that you would like students to work on and, if it is too long to write on the board, make a class set of copies.
2   Leaf through glossy magazines with interesting photographs in and find a picture that seems in some way to relate to the poem. Do not analyse your choice too much. Select almost unconsciously anything that seems to relate to the poem by colour or shape or story or mood. Make enough copies of the picture for students to be able to have a good look at it from quite close up.

Procedure
1 Display or hand out pictures along with copies of the poem. Allow students time to read the poem and study the picture.
2 Ask students to discuss in pairs any similarities they see between the poem and the picture and to write down their ideas.
3 Ask students to tell the whole class what similarities they have found.

Follow on
In later lessons, ask students to find pictures that go with any text or poem that they have been working with lately in class. Either ask them to state the reason they chose the pictures or let them ask you what similarities *you* see.

Variations
• If you have no colour photocopier, find several different pictures that could equally well go with the poem.
• If you think the poem is likely to prove challenging to your students, do basic work on its meaning earlier in the same lesson or in a previous lesson.

Comment
One aim of this activity is to help students notice ideas and images in the poem. Another is to wake up their metaphoric intelligence.

Tessa Woodward

8.11 From sketch to discussion of a short story

Age	13 and up
Level	Lower-intermediate–Advanced
Time	15–25 minutes
Focus	Post-reading discussion of a short story
Material	A class set of a short story, ideally one whose events take place in just two or three locations, e.g. the beginning in one place and the end in another

Preparation
1 Make a class set of copies of the story along with a fairly detailed set of comprehension questions.
2 Assign the reading as homework. You can either hand out the questions at the same time (to be answered as homework) or hand them out just after Step 3. In the latter case, the activity will take longer than indicated above.

Procedure

1   If the story has two main locations, divide the class into A and B halves; if three locations, then into ABC thirds (and adjust Steps 2–5 accordingly).

2   Say that each of the A students should sketch the first location and each of the Bs, the last location. Ask them to include all the important people and things plus any labels they think might be helpful, e.g. the name of a person, words for key objects, an important verb that someone else in the class might not know. (As students draw, encourage them to look at the drawings being made by others in their half of the class and say that they should copy any ideas they like.)

3   Ask the class to form pairs such that one partner comes from the A half and the other partner from the B half of the class.

4   Each A shows her sketch to B and explains it in as much detail as she can. When she has no more to say, B says anything he remembers or thinks about A's part of the story which she forgot. Then B and A talk about B's sketch in the same way.

5   With the same partner(s), students go through the comprehension questions, skipping any which they are sure they have already answered in the course of their discussion. Remind students that they can call you over if there is a question they cannot answer.

Follow on

Ask the class if there are any outstanding questions.

Variation

In Step 2, students work in pairs and produce one sketch per pair. Try to arrange things so that your least proficient students each work with someone who is a bit stronger than them (but not one who is vastly stronger). Then, in Step 3, pairs sit with pairs, e.g. AA with BB.

Tip

Step 2: Even if you decide that everyone should draw his or her own sketch, encourage students to work in pairs or small groups. This enables them to share ideas both about the story and about how to produce adequate sketches.

Comment

This activity is a good one to use if you have assigned a short story but some students have not read it – they can sit with others who have and, generally, learn quite a bit.

Usable short stories
'While the Auto Waits' and 'The Last Leaf' by O. Henry, 'The Story Teller' and 'The Open Window' by Saki, 'Lispeth' by Rudyard Kipling and 'The Man from the South' by Roald Dahl. (Stories by 19th- and early 20th-century authors, e.g. Poe, O. Henry, Saki, Kipling, are often available on the Internet. You can download them and abridge them for intermediate learners.)

Seth Lindstromberg

8.12 Literature interpretation mandala

Age	12 and up
Level	Intermediate–Advanced
Time	30–45 minutes
Focus	Post-reading discussion of short stories or poems
Material	Black and white photocopies of one or more mandalas, crayons or coloured pencils

Preparation
Use the mandala shown below or choose one or some from one of the mandala books on the market or check out a mandala website.

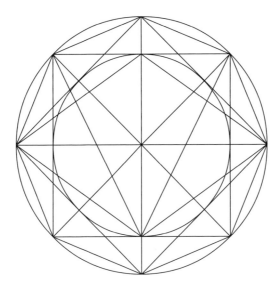

Procedure
1   Give out your mandala(s) immediately after the class has finished reading the poem or story.

2   Ask students each to colour in a mandala in a way which expresses the feelings that the poem or story aroused in them. Tell them to position their strongest and most important feelings in or around the centre of the mandala and other, weaker feelings around the edge.

3   Ask your students to:
    a   pair up and discuss what they have coloured and why
    b   leave their first partner, find a new one, and discuss again
    c   find a third partner and discuss a third time

4   Bring the class back together for a plenary discussion. Elicit interpretations. As different points are made, write fairly full notes (or complete sentences) on the board.

5   Students copy what is on the board into their notebooks.

Variations
• Step 2: Say that they can also write words, but only a few.
• Ask upper-intermediate and advanced students each to fill in a mandala about the main protagonist. They may place the name of the protagonist in the centre and build a character sketch by placing around the name notes and labels about this person's nature and actions. Again, nearness to the name in the centre should reflect the importance given to any comment or label. In a highly mixed proficiency class, these students will be able to contribute to the various discussions in a different way than the others.

Jean Rüdiger-Harper

8.13 Summarap

Age	12–18
Level	Intermediate–Advanced
Time	45 minutes for Steps 1–7, Step 8 in a later lesson
Focus	Post-reading summarising of a literary work, listening, pronunciation in general and rhythm in particular, writing rap lyrics
Material	A recording of a good English rap song; a class set of the lyrics, an audio cassette/CD player, (optional) a few tambourines or similar

Preparation
Find a suitable rap song. (Perhaps ask students to loan you some of their favourite recordings.)

Procedure

LESSON 1

1 Pre-teach any necessary vocabulary.
2 Play the recording.
3 Elicit opinions about the main story line and discuss its meaning.
4 Make sure everyone is clear about the beat. For example, ask them to beat or tap it out as you replay a bit of it.
5 Practise saying the rap with students, first chorally, and then in pairs.
6 Ask the students to compose a short rap about the piece of literature they have just read, which is to include the main story line and any other comments they care to make, using the rhythm and beat of the rap they have just practised. Let the students choose whether to work in groups, pairs or individually.
7 Ask them to perfect their lyrics and their performances for homework.

LESSON 2

8 Students perform their raps.

Variations
• Stop after Step 6.
• Suggest that students use tambourines or other simple percussion instruments.

Jean Rüdiger-Harper

8.14 Card quiz game on a novel

Age	15 and up
Level	Intermediate–Upper-intermediate
Time	45 minutes (this usually allows the groups to play the game twice)
Focus	Reviewing a fairly long literary text, reading, speaking
Material	A set of cards (see below) plus (optionally) a die for every group, small objects as counters, one sheet of A3 paper for each group, small prizes, e.g. seedless grapes, small chocolates

Preparation

Make up sets of three or four dozen questions about the text (novel, short story or long poem such as 'The Rime of the Ancient Mariner') and write each one on a card. Perhaps include a few cards saying *Collect a prize* and also a few bearing general knowledge questions with no connection to the text or ones such as *What is the date of our next test?*

Procedure

1 Divide the class into groups of four or five and say that they are going to play a game to review what they have just read. Make sure that each group has at least one copy of the novel or short story being reviewed.

2 Give each group a set of cards to be placed face down in a pile in the middle of the group.

3 In turn, each player takes a card and tries to answer the question that is on it. If they can, they get the card. If they cannot, or if they get the question wrong (the other players have to judge), they put the card back face down at the bottom of the pile. The game goes on until all the cards have been collected, or the group is left with one or more that nobody can answer – at which point they ask you what the answers are to the cards they did not know. The winner is the one with the most cards at the end of the game.

Variation

More elaborately, give each group a 'board' (on A3 paper), a die, and, for each player, a counter (e.g. a button, small piece of wood or coloured cloth). The board consists of a serpentine route with a beginning and an end. Between the beginning and the end are 60 or so numbered 'squares', of which about 17 are black and the rest white, as on p. 187. Students take turns throwing the die and move along the route accordingly, e.g. four squares if the die shows 4. The player who has just moved takes a card on which is a 'snakes and ladders'-type statement or question such as (about the novel *Wuthering Heights*): *Heathcliff's dogs chase you. Go back four* or *Lockwood invites you to dinner, but you do not want to go. Think up a good excuse or go back four* or *Collect a prize* (including prize cards adds fun and competitiveness to the game).

Comment

The materials may be time-consuming to create but they can be used again and again, so the initial effort is worthwhile.

Jean Rüdiger-Harper

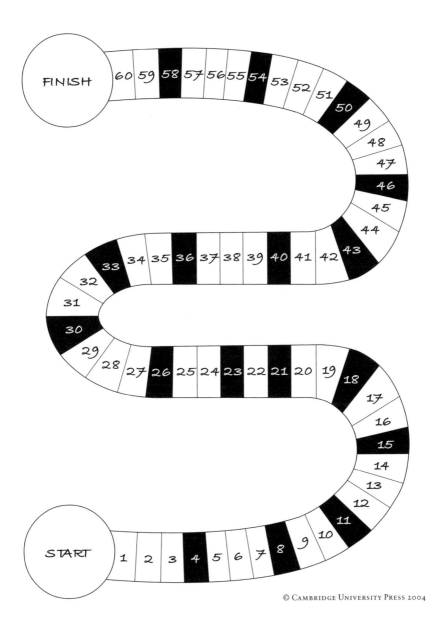

8.15 Two short texts on a similar topic

Age	13 and up
Level	Pre-intermediate–Advanced
Time	25–35 minutes
Focus	Reading and discussing two short texts
Material	Two poems, lyrics or very short stories on class sets of handouts

A good lead-in to this activity is 'Comparing it and me' (2.7).

Preparation

Choose two similar texts, e.g. 'A Visit to the Asylum' (p. 173) and 'It was long ago' (below). Prepare enough handouts for everyone to have one. The texts can be on the same or on different sheets.

Procedure

1   Give everyone a copy of both texts and allow time for reading.
2   Ask your class to get together in twos or threes and make a list of 12 (or so) things that the two texts have in common and another list, at least half as long, of differences. The students work together to produce the lists, but each student must make a copy for use in Step 4.
3   Ask the pairs or threesomes to split up and form new groups of three or four students who did not work together in Step 2.
4   In each group, students compare their lists.
5   Bring the class together and ask students to tell you the most interesting comments they heard *someone else* make.

Variation
Use texts that are not of the same type, e.g. a poem and a song lyric.

Ages 15 and up, Intermediate–Advanced:

It was long ago (Eleanor Farjeon)

I'll tell you, shall I, something I remember?
Something that still means a great deal to me.
It was long ago.

A dusty road in summer I remember,
A mountain, and an old house, and a tree
That stood, you know,

Behind the house. An old woman I remember
In a red shawl with a grey cat on her knee
Humming under a tree.

She seemed the oldest thing I can remember,
But then perhaps I was not more than three.
It was long ago.

I dragged on the dusty road, and I remember
How the old woman looked over the fence at me
And seemed to know

How it felt to be three, and called out, I remember,
"Do you like bilberries and cream for tea?"
I went under the tree

And while she hummed, and the cat purred, I remember
How she filled a saucer with berries and cream for me
So long ago.

Such berries and such cream as I remember,
I never had seen before and never see
Today, you know.

And that is almost all I can remember,
The house, the mountain, the grey cat on her knee,
Her red shawl, and the tree.

And the taste of the berries, the feel of the sun I remember,
And the smell of everything that used to be
So long ago,

Till the heat on the road outside again I remember,
And how the long dusty road seemed to have for me
No end, you know.

That is the farthest thing I can remember.
It won't mean much to you. It does to me.
Then I grew up, you see.

Other usable pairs of poems
- Look for pairs of poems on the Internet by doing a search on 'love poems', 'moon poems', 'cat poems', 'sea poems', 'poems about anger' and so on. (You can often find collections posted by students in school English classes.)
- Ages 14 and up, Upper-intermediate–Advanced: 'Symphony in Yellow' by Oscar Wilde and 'Composed upon Westminster Bridge, September 3, 1802' by William Wordsworth. (Both on the Internet.)
- Ages 16 and up, Intermediate–Advanced: Various tree poems by Robert Frost, e.g. 'Gathering leaves', 'Leaf treader', 'Pea brush', 'In hardwood groves', 'Tree at my window', 'Now close the windows', 'The sound of trees' (*Selected Poems*. 1973. Penguin.)

Seth Lindstromberg

Activities elsewhere in this book that are usable with literary texts

3.11 (A specific story or poem can be one of the topics that students speak about), 3.14 (Students can quiz each other about a literary text), 4.6 (Use a medium-length poem that is not too complex syntactically or conceptually), 4.7 (Use a recording of a relatively easy poem), 5.2 (Use a short literary text on a particular topic), 5.4 (Use a short poem), 5.7–5.9 (Use narrative poems or very short stories), 9.3 (Hand out true statements relating to a story or novel students have read)

9 Building the skills of discussion and debate

THE VALUE OF DEBATE AS A CLASSROOM ACTIVITY

Students, especially ones who are relatively well-motivated, frequently say they want to discuss or debate issues that are of genuine interest to them. This must partly be so because the idea of discussing and debating issues of consequence is in tune with teenage idealism. Another factor may be a growing desire on the part of many teens to experiment with adult-like ways of relating to others, and the activities of discussing and debating have very adult auras. However, successful discussions depend on a range of skills which young people may need to acquire in a largely step-by-step fashion. This is even truer of successful debates. The skills in question are ones which few 16-year olds, let alone younger pupils, have much mastery of.

That is where the activities in this chapter come in. All can play a role in developing skills required for successful discussing and debating. The chapter culminates with a full-scale debate activity (9.11, 'Single switch debating'). Aside from being useful in themselves, these activities form potential stepping stones for any of your students who may wish to go further: into the world of extra-curricular club debates in the Oxford style (i.e. based on academic disputation), Parliamentary style (i.e. based on House of Commons debating), and Cross-Examination style (i.e. based on courtroom interrogation).

In some countries, classroom debate remains virtually unknown. In others it has been established for generations as an extra-curricular, club-type activity and/or as a fixed part of the regular curriculum. There are yet other countries in which debating has become popular only recently. Among these are various recent and prospective members of the European Union as well as other relatively young or aspiring democracies around the world. In such lands debating is often seen by government officials, community and business leaders, educators, and parents as a means of:

- familiarising young people with the everyday practice of democratic governance
- imparting social and forensic skills key to success as a civil servant, lawyer, politician or businessperson

- broadening and strengthening connections with the international community

A further reason for the increased interest in debate is the very widespread desire on the part of governments and parents to have young people learn English at much earlier ages than before. Debating in the schools, *in English*, puts all these things together rather neatly. A clear case would be the members of a school debating team who win through to be selected to compete abroad where they would have excellent opportunities to form personal connections with politically-engaged young people from other countries. But to one degree or another the advantages of learning how to debate can apply to everyone.

Let us look at five broad areas in which personal development can occur through learning to debate.

SOCIAL INTEGRATION

Debaters must be able to work independently yet also as part of a team. To do the latter, they must listen well, follow rules and show respect for other participants, e.g. the Chair or the moderator (i.e. manager) of a debate and the members of the opposing team. Debaters are obliged to learn how to maintain self-control and be courteous in any discussion.

INTELLECTUAL DEVELOPMENT

Debaters must be able to relate specific points to generalisations and, to support generalisations, they must be able to refer to pertinent examples. They must be able to understand an assertion as a whole, recognise its key terms and recognise or think of facts that support or undermine it. They must know how to construct and state arguments, and how to memorise key material (e.g. numbers and pertinent quotations).

STUDY SKILLS

They must be able both to plan research and to carry it out: to sift, record, and marshal information.

VERBAL SELF-EXPRESSION

They need to learn to speak fluently and confidently in longer turns and, when speaking, stick to a topic and generally be relevant. They must be able to challenge and defend positions, and to use both humour and figurative language constructively. They must be able to deliver their ideas effectively with, for instance, good eye contact, well-timed gestures, good voice control and an ability to pause for dramatic effect.

RESPECT FOR CORE TENETS OF DISCUSSION IN A
REPRESENTATIVE DEMOCRACY

They must commit to rational argument and renounce emotional demagoguery and any use of invented facts and other lies. They must be open to the view that controversial assertions can be rationally examined and discussed.

Again, these abilities, or skills, are not ones of use only to top rank debaters. Many are part of being a useful citizen (e.g. being able to recognise the key terms in a statement and being able to follow rules). Others are also valuable to anyone who communicates with others (e.g. being able to stick to a topic when speaking and to be passionate without losing self-control). Taken together, these skills approach being a recipe for the opportunity to be prominently successful in later life. Indeed, for certain countries where formal debating has been established for some time, lists of well-known figures in business, government and academe who debated while in school or university are very long indeed.

Fluency under pressure and other prerequisites of debating

9.1 Timed topic talks

Age	13 and up
Level	Upper-elementary–Advanced
Time	5–25 minutes, depending on the variation used
Focus	Oral fluency, sticking to a topic while speaking for a minute or more

This is a good follow on from 'Letter on the board' (3.11) and '30-second stimulus talks' (3.12).

Procedure

1 In order to give students an idea of how much there can be to say about a simple topic, give a one-minute talk on some such topic as coffee. Say one or two things about a number of aspects of the topic. When you finish, ask the class to recall and tell back to you ten things you said.

2 If you have an even number of students, divide them into A/B pairs. If you have an odd number, see the first Variation below.

3 Say that you will call out a topic such as one of those listed on p. 195. Tell your class that:

- When you say *Go!*, the As will have, say, 60 seconds (vary the time with level) to talk about the topic.
- When the set time is up, you will call out *B!* and the Bs must continue talking about the *same* topic for another minute (or whatever seems appropriate).

4 Bring the class together. Ask some or all students to say *one* thing they remember their partner saying. (Students generally report the most interesting thing without being specifically asked to do this.)

Follow on

- After your students have had some experience doing this activity in pairs, divide the class into groups of three or four. In each group one student at a time speaks on a *different* topic for, say, at least 1½ minutes but no more than 4 minutes. Speakers must begin by saying something such as:

    I'm very pleased to be here today. My topic is . . . Could you please save any questions till the end?

    On finishing they should say something like:

    Oh! It looks like my time's up. Such a pity! Are there any (more) questions? OK. Well, thank you for your attention. Now over to . . .

    Write these frames on the board. Note, students will need to take turns being time-keeper for whoever is speaking.

- Students speak in larger and larger groups and eventually they take turns speaking to the whole class for a set time: one or two speakers per lesson.

Variations

- If you have an odd number of students, form one or more threesomes in which one student is A, one B and one C. Everyone else pairs up. In each pair, one student is B and the other is *both* A *and* C. Then do as in Step 3 above except that when the B time limit is up, call out *C!* All the Cs have to speak, on the same topic, for a further set time. Of course that means that in the pairs, the A/C students speak twice. Tell them this beforehand.
- Gradually extend the time limits.
- Put students in mixed proficiency A/B/C threesomes. Set a low time limit for each turn. When everyone has had their turn to speak, announce that there is a further minute (or whatever) during which anyone in the threesome can say something else they would have said if they had had more time.

- Add 'tell back' stages. That is, after A has spoken, B tries to tell A everything he or she said. Then vice versa. (Thanks to Mario Rinvolucri for this idea.)

Tips
- Step 1: With some topics, it may help to quickly pre-teach a bit of vocabulary. For example, if your topic is 'Teeth in general or yours in particular', at lower levels especially it may be helpful to draw on the board a tooth and add such labels as: *root*, *gum*, *cavity* and *filling*. But going too far with this can leave students feeling there is little left for them to say.
- Step 1: A very common student mistake is to use the singular instead of the plural when the topic is, say, 'Bananas'. That is, students may say *I like it very much*. To help forestall such errors, write a reminder on the board just before the speaking phase, something like this:

    bananas → they, them

    Elicit three or four statements about bananas using *they* or *them*.

Comment
An ideal topic is one about which there is little risk in expressing an opinion. There must also be a good deal of common ground between partners. It is probably for this reason that topics like 'My favourite place' tend not to work so well. For controversial topics, other frameworks work better – the debate framework, for example. ('Beggars' is the nearest thing to a controversial topic I have found to work as a 'timed topic talk'.)

Topics

potatoes	bananas	cockroaches
bees	mosquitoes	eggs
chocolate	a favourite pair of shoes	beggars
spiders	fizzy drinks	junk food
the moon	riding on a bus	karaoke
mobile phones	city parks	being at a beach

apples (or some other locally common fruit)
teeth in general or yours in particular
socks in general and/or a favourite pair
hair in general or yours in particular

Seth Lindstromberg

9.2 Pro and con presentations

Age	14 and up
Level	Intermediate–Advanced
Time	5 minutes to explain what to do, plus time for research and time for the talks (at least 3 minutes per talk), more than one lesson
Focus	Planning and giving a short pro and con talk, phrases and sentences for structuring the talk and managing discussion, political awareness
Material	A class set of 'Instructions for moderators' (p. 198)

Preparation

1　Every nation produces towering figures who nevertheless make mistakes, at least in the eyes of some. For Britain, Winston Churchill and Margaret Thatcher are two who spring to mind. Think of at least three such figures whom all of your students are likely to know something about. Do not include figures who are generally thought of as being virtual saints or as being completely evil.

2　On the board (or on an OHP transparency) write a discourse skeleton such as the following:

My subject is ....

Many people think that .... because ....

.... and because ....

However, I think that ....

because .... and because ....

In short, ... because ....

Separated from the skeleton, add one of these 'sentence heads':

Also, ... Additionally,............................ .

Procedure

EXPLAINING WHAT TO DO

1　Ask your students to pair up.

2　If you have thought of three controversial figures, form groups of three pairs each. (Put four pairs in each group if you have thought of four figures.)

3 Assign figures to different pairs within the groups and say that:
   - each pair is going to prepare a talk about their prominent figure using the talk frame on the board
   - they should first decide whether they mostly approve or disapprove of this person. If they approve, they should put any negative points that they think of in the first half of the frame; if they *dis*approve, then vice versa.
   - they should note their ideas (not in complete sentences) on another sheet of paper
   - partners need to decide who is going to say which part(s) of the talk
   - there will be a 'moderator' (i.e. a discussion manager) in each group. Add that this role will shift from person to person during the talks.
   - the moderator will always be a student who is not a member of the pair whose turn it is to speak. Students should decide who is going to be the moderator for each pair.
4 Hand out the moderator instructions (on p. 198) and ask everyone to read them.

RESEARCH

5 Tell everyone that now they need to do some research, e.g. in a library, by using the Internet, and through asking friends, relatives and others about their figure.

THE TALKS

6 Re-form the groups created in Step 2 and decide which pairs will speak in what order. Before starting the talks, stress that the listeners should ask questions and comment after each talk.
7 Have the students present their talks, within their groups.
8 When the talks are finished, bring the class together and, for each prominent figure, elicit all the strengths and weaknesses that were mentioned in the different groups.

Follow on
Ask pairs (or individuals) each to write a version of their talk better than the one they actually gave.

Variations
- Students give the talks individually.
- Students speak to the whole class. (This works best if each pair has a different figure to talk about.)

- As topics, choose products, institutions, practices, customs and states of affairs that have a bright and a dark side, e.g. the car, television, school, school uniforms, divorce, tourism, modern life.
- After doing some or all of activities 9.3–9.11, stage 'controversial figure' debates in which (after sufficient time for research and preparation) one pair stresses the accomplishments of a prominent person and the other, his or her mistakes, as follows: (1) A moderator introduces the panelists. (2) The pro team speaks for a fixed amount of time (e.g. two minutes), setting out their basic position with reasons. (3) The con team speaks for the same amount of time, also setting out their basic position. (4) The pro team responds to the con team's arguments (e.g. 1½ minutes). (5) The con team gets the same amount of time to respond. (6) The pro team gets a minute to summarise their position in light of what the other team has said. (7) The con team has a minute to summarise. (8) The moderator elicits questions from the floor and finally thanks all participants and brings the debate to a close.

Instructions for moderators

- If you are the first moderator for the first pair to speak, welcome everybody and introduce the first pair of speakers:
  a   *Welcome, everyone. I'm so glad you could all come today.*
  b   *First to speak are .... and ....*
  c   *May I ask who you are going to talk about?*
  d   *Excellent. So, everyone, let's give them a warm welcome.*
- When they finish speaking, you say:
  e   *Thank you very much, ... and ....*
  f   *Let's have some questions from the audience.*
  g   *Right, let's finish there. .... and ...., thank you very much for agreeing to speak to us today.*
  h   *Now, who is the next moderator?*
- If you are the second moderator, do not say (a). Begin by saying:
  b   *Next to speak are .... and ....*
  Then go on to (c), etc.
- If you are the moderator for the last pair, do the same, but instead of (h) say:
  i   *That's the end of this series of talks. Now I will wave to [teacher's name] to show that we've finished.*

Comment

The technique of giving students a discourse skeleton is extremely adaptable (see also 3.13, 'Pitching a wonderful new product'). For a given topic, you can script skeletons which are quite detailed or ones which are decidedly spare, as appropriate to the level of your students.

Seth Lindstromberg

9.3 Challenge the assertion!

Age	13 and up
Level	Lower-intermediate–Advanced
Time	15–20 minutes
Focus	Critical thinking, challenging and justifying assertions, fluency
Material	For each student, a slip bearing a few statements (see p. 201)

Preparation

Make enough copies of the statement box (p. 201) for half the class and then cut the copies so that the left and right columns are separate.

Procedure

1 Write the question box on the board and explain that (1) the questions top left are ones we ask when someone says something and we want to find out why they believe it and (2) those top right are ones we ask when we want to know how their statement is important.

The question box

About reasons for believing:

– Why do you **think** so?
– What's your **evi**dence for that?
– What makes you say **that**?

When you want more details about a reason:

– Can you explain **why**?
– Can you be more spe**cif**ic?

About importance:

– How is that **good/bad**?
– How is **that** important?
– Why does **that** matter?

When you want another reason:

– Give me another reason why . . .

© CAMBRIDGE UNIVERSITY PRESS 2004

---

2 Form your class into A/B pairs and give each partner a different half of the statement box.

- Explain that in a minute, in each pair, Student A will say one of their statements.
- Student B responds with one of the questions on the board.
- Student A replies with a justification.
- B queries the justification by asking the same question again or by asking a different one of the questions on the board and so on until ideas run out.
- When ideas do run out, A and B change roles.

Offer something like the dialogue below as an example, but add that even an exchange as short as ABA is satisfactory. (Your better motivated students are not likely to need much prompting to have longer dialogues than that.)

A: *It's a nice day today.*
B: *What's your evidence for that?*
A: *The sun is shining.*
B: *How is that good?*
A: *We need sunshine.*
B: *Can you explain why?*
A: *We become sad without the sun.*
B: *Give me another reason why we need sunshine.*
A: *Plants need the sun.*
B: *How is that important?*
A: *Enough. Let's swap.*

3   Give the signal to start the dialogues.

Follow on

In the same lesson or in a later one, give out (or elicit) lists of controversial assertions for students to work with: *Fraud damages society*, *The rich should give most of their money to charity*, *Over-population is a threat to the planet*, *Nurses deserve more money than company presidents* (or vice versa), *Some films and video games are harmful*.

Variations

- Students do not form stable pairs but instead mill around the room as if at a cocktail party.
- To make the activity even more doable by low-proficient students, put students in groups of four. In each group, Students A and B are a team against C and D. Student A reads out a statement. Either C or D can reply. To this, either A or B can reply and so on.

- Subtract items from the question box according to level, or add some (e.g. *I'm not sure I see why*).

Tips
- Step 2: Stress that B does *not* make statements but only asks questions. *Stress also that whoever gets a statement should try to defend it regardless of their own opinions.* (This is a vital element of club debating generally.)
- Step 3: One way of motivating students is to say that Person A is in the role of witness at a trial while Person B is in the role of highly sceptical barrister.
- It may be a good idea to work with relatively few controversial statements in the context of this activity. The reason for this is that students may feel that any issues covered in this activity have been 'done', and this feeling may reduce their motivation to work with any of these issues in later, full-scale debating lessons.

Comment
By asking students to work with relatively uncontroversial statements, you lessen the risk that students who disagree passionately about a sensitive issue will lose track of a key purpose of the activity, which is to broaden everyone's repertoire of ways of challenging and defending assertions.

The statement box

Hair is useful.
Prisons are necessary.
For a working person, cats are better pets than dogs.
It's useful to be able to speak a few languages.
Taxes are necessary.
Science has given us a lot.
Drug addiction is bad.
Inexpensive public transport is necessary.
Women are more law-abiding than men.
Caring for a baby can be time-consuming.

Trees are beneficial.
Sunshine is beneficial.
Doctors do a lot of good.
Exercise is beneficial.
Rats are pests.
Car racing is a dangerous sport.
Everyone should brush their teeth.
Every house needs a roof.
Shoes are useful.
People should eat less junk food.
School is useful.

Seth Lindstromberg

9.4 Just a minute!

Age	11 and up
Level	Intermediate–Advanced
Time	20–30 minutes
Focus	Sticking to a topic, challenging a speaker, following rules, keeping track of time, fluency
Material	A timepiece of some kind which tells seconds

Preparation

Draw up a list of topics that have come up recently in your coursebook, during class work or in your school generally, so that students will be likely to have plenty of ideas of what to say, e.g. school lunches, coming to school in the morning, watching television, things people do during their holidays, visiting relatives. (See also the topic box on page 195.)

Procedure

1   Divide the class into teams of four or five people.
2   Explain the rules and reason for playing the game.
   a   One person in a team gets a topic. At the word *Start*, they have to talk to the whole class about that topic for as long as possible up to a minute.
   b   If nobody from another team challenges them and they finish the minute, they get ten points. (But if they do not finish the minute, even if they finish in 59 seconds, they get no points.)
   c   Members of other teams can challenge the speaker by saying *Challenge!* The challenger must give a reason, for example:
       • *False! We did not have spaghetti yesterday.*
       • *Grammar! She said, 'Yesterday I have been . . .'. The grammar is wrong.*
       • *Not relevant! The topic is school lunches, not her favourite food.*
       • *Pronunciation! Not* ho**tel**, **ho**tel.
       • *Repetition! You said that before.*
   d   A correct challenge brings the challenger one point for their team. Challengers who can correct a speaker's mistake get two additional points for their team.
   e   No points are lost for incorrect challenges. If the challenge is incorrect, the original speaker continues with the same topic, trying to finish their minute.

f   If they cannot correct the utterance, other teams have a chance to do so and if they succeed, they get one point.

g   When challenged, a speaker must pause and wait until the challenge has been discussed.

h   The clock 'stops' while a challenge is being discussed. (If you do not have a stopwatch, each time there is a challenge, quickly note how many seconds the speaker had been speaking up to then so you know how many seconds are left when you start again.)

i   The challenger himself or herself does not have to take on the job of continuing to speak on the topic; some other member of his or her team can do this if they wish.

j   If the original speaker had spoken for ten seconds before being challenged, the new team takes on the same topic but just for fifty seconds.

k   The game continues with the original topic being passed from team to team every time there is a correct challenge and for a shorter and shorter time each time until the minute runs out.

l   Whoever is speaking when the minute is up gains ten points for their team.

m   Once the points are all recorded for that round, a new topic is started with the second team.

Follow on

As the class get better at doing the game, you can extend the categories of challenge to include, for example, hesitation of more than three seconds.

Tip

Step 2c: If confidence in speaking is a problem for many of your students, do not introduce all of these categories of challenge right away; for instance, bring in grammar and pronunciation challenges a bit later on.

Comment

Debaters need to stay with a topic while speaking under the double pressure of a time limit and the likelihood that they will be challenged by the opposing side. This is a fun way of giving students practice in speaking while under similar pressure.

Acknowledgement

This is an adaptation of a popular radio show of the same name (BBC Radio 4). Cassettes are commercially available.

Tessa Woodward

Additional prerequisites of debating

9.5 Collecting small-scale debate topics

Age	13 and up
Level	Intermediate–Advanced
Time	10 minutes
Focus	Topics for mini-debates
Material	A large sheet of poster paper

Procedure

1 Give some examples of small, everyday topics which you think your students would have plenty to say about, e.g. tattoos, body piercing and flared jeans (or some other clothing style).

2 Put your sheet of poster paper up on the wall and prepare to write the topics on it. Ask the students to think about what they were talking about in the last break or lunch hour and then call out to you any topics they think might be suitable. Write any reasonable suggestion onto the poster.

3 Say that everyone must come to the next lesson with one more small topic they think the class could have fun discussing.

Tips
- Step 1: If you have already done '30-second stimulus talks' (3.12) or 'Just a minute!' (9.4), explain that you need some *new* topics.
- Step 1: Add that although doing big topics like crime and pollution is very worthwhile, doing a good deal of specialist vocabulary and research is required in order to cover them well. Explain that you would like to build up a list of smaller topics that would be both relatively easy and amusing for them to discuss without the necessity of doing a lot of research just yet.

Tessa Woodward

9.6 Exploring small-scale debate topics

Age	13 and up
Level	Intermediate–Advanced
Time	5–10 minutes each time over a series of lessons
Focus	Discovery of multiple facets of a single topic, discussing
Material	A large sheet of poster paper

An effective debater expects that topics that are quite simple on the surface can have many facets. A key purpose of this activity is to make students more aware of this. It is a good follow on from 'Collecting small-scale debate topics' (9.5).

Procedure

1 Write a topic on the board (e.g. *mobile phones*) and write it in the centre of the board with spokes radiating out from it. At the end of each spoke, write a question, e.g. *What are they made of?*, *Where do they come from?*, *Convenience?*, *Problems?*, *Personal experience?*, *Who needs them most?*, *When shouldn't you use one?*, *What did people do before there were mobile phones?*, *Who doesn't like them?*

2 Ask students if they can suggest any other questions. For *mobile phones* you might get: *Cost?* and *Appearance?*

3 Put students into groups of three or four and ask them to explore the topic (in this case, *mobile phones*) by providing at least one answer to each question.

4 When groups seem to have covered most of the spokes, bring the class back together and ask if anyone raised an aspect of the topic not covered by any of the spokes. For instance, one group might say they had been discussing the theft of mobile phones from people in the street. If so, add another spoke and label it appropriately, e.g. *Recent developments* or *Crime*.

Tip
Step 2: To save space, abbreviate the questions as much as possible.
Step 4: Keep a copy of your board work so you can refer to it later on when reviewing vocabulary or if (when preparing the class for a formal discussion or debate) you want to remind the class how much there is to talk about in connection with an apparently small topic as you move closer to doing more traditional discussions and debates. (One option is to photograph such key board work; another is to use not the board but an OHP and keep your transparency.)

Follow on/Variation
On a subsequent occasion (or as a Variation with relatively intellectual students), build up a mind-map (see 5.1).

Acknowledgement
Thanks to Larry Cole for the idea of the potential of small topics.

Tessa Woodward

9.7 Controversy role plays

Age	13 and up
Level	Intermediate–Advanced
Time	30–40 minutes
Focus	Brainstorming ideas, arguing your side, listening closely to other people's arguments and learning to counter them
Material	Class sets of cards for a two-role role play

Procedure

1 Introduce a topic such as 'the life cycle of a butterfly'.

2 On the board sketch the various stages of a butterfly's life: egg, caterpillar, chrysalis, butterfly.

3 Elicit or teach important associated nouns (*leaf*, *cocoon*, etc.) and verbs (*lay*, *hatch*, etc.). Check understanding and write up these words as you go along.

4 Form an even number of groups of four or five people. Some groups will prepare according to Role A and an equal number of groups will prepare according to Role B. Say that in a minute they will all be caterpillars.

5 Hand out the role cards. Put a red spot in a corner of all the A cards and a green spot in a corner of all the B cards.

EXAMPLE CARDS

Role A

You are a caterpillar. You love being a caterpillar. You do not want to change into a chrysalis or become a butterfly. In your group, think of all the reasons you can why:

- it is good to be a caterpillar (e.g. *You can eat as much as you like, You don't have to worry about your figure.*)
- you think it would be terrible to be a butterfly (e.g. *People might catch you and pin you on a board.*)

Role B

You are a caterpillar. You hate being a caterpillar. You are longing to turn into a chrysalis and then become a butterfly. In your group, think of all the reasons you can why:

- it is terrible being a caterpillar (e.g. *When you walk too far, you get blisters on all your many feet.*)
- it would be wonderful to be a butterfly (e.g. *You could fly up and look through people's windows.*)

Tell the class their ideas can be as crazy and as funny as they like. Add that every student in every group needs to write down all the ideas produced by their group.

6 Start the group work. Mingle and help out with vocabulary and ideas.

7 When everyone has several ideas noted down, ask them to notice the colour of the spot on their role card.

8 Students leave their groups (taking their notes with them) and sit opposite someone from a group whose card had a different colour on it (i.e. red sits opposite green and vice versa).

9 Say something like this: *Imagine you are green caterpillars each sitting on a leaf in the sunshine. You have your head down munching away. All of a sudden you notice there is another caterpillar on the same leaf munching its way towards you. You stop, say* Hello, *and start talking about how you feel about being a caterpillar. Munch, munch, go!*

10 Allow time for the caterpillars to talk to each other.

11 Students, *in note form*, write down the reasons given by the other caterpillar.

12 Tell them they now need to think how they can counter each reason or argument in their next conversation with another caterpillar of the same opinion as the first one they talked to.

13 Ask red-spot caterpillars to stay seated and green-spot ones to move a couple of desks away so that new green/red pairs are formed.

14 Ask the new pairs to have conversations that are longer and better than they had the first time.

Variations

The same basic procedure can be used with any two-part role play that has a built-in difference of opinion:

> - two pet birds in a cage (or lions in a zoo): one wants to stay; one wants to escape
> - two tigers: one wants to become a vegetarian; the other does not
> - two siblings: one wants to leave home; the other wants to live with Mum and Dad 'forever'
> - two siblings who share a room: one likes music (or likes everything in its place, or wants to be rich and famous); one likes silence (or hates putting things away, or wants to live an ordinary life)
> - two siblings: one wants to work for a living; the other wants to live on the dole forever
> - two students who are about to graduate: one is keen to leave school; one wants to stay (Perhaps, as a lead-in to this last scenario, mention the case of an American man of about 25 who, in the late 1990s, moved to a new town, impersonated a teenager, enrolled in a local high school and was very popular with everyone – until his deception was discovered.)
> - two porpoises find a human in danger of drowning: one wants to save the human; the other does not
> - the president/prime minister of a country and a top adviser are considering whether to have a space exploration programme or not: one is in favour; one is not
> - two scientists who have accidentally discovered the secret of eternal life and eternal youth: one wants to publicise the information; the other believes it is a horrible discovery and thinks they should never tell their secret to anyone

Acknowledgement

I learned this activity from Tom Hunter at South Devon Technical College in 1984.

Tessa Woodward

9.8 The PMI brainstorm

Age	11 and up
Level	Intermediate–Advanced
Time	20–30 minutes
Focus	Thinking skills

This activity introduces students to a particularly useful set of criteria for selecting and categorising information found when doing research.

Procedure

1 Say that you are now going to teach them another way of building up a broad range of ideas: the 'PMI way' (i.e. the Plus, Minus, Interesting way). Explain that you can use this method when you have a strong emotional reaction to a topic or suggestion such as this one: *All boys should wear skirts*. Tell your class that they might immediately think that this is a terrible, crazy or stupid idea but add that this is what makes it an opinion to think about in the PMI way.

2 Divide the board into three columns headed, respectively, *P*, *M* and *I*.

3 Elicit the good things about the idea of boys wearing skirts and write them up in the *P* column. For example, *Skirts are easier to make than trousers*. Once you have several ideas, move to the *M* column and elicit and write up bad things about the idea. For example, *You can't take long steps*. Once you have several ideas in this column, move to the *I* column. Now you want things that people find interesting about the idea. For example, in many countries around the world men wear 'sort of' skirts such as sarongs, kilts and (men's) kimonos.

4 Once students have got the idea of how to do a PMI, take a fresh topic such as the following: *All students should get two days off from school a year to attend events connected with their hobbies*. Ask students to work individually, make PMI columns in their notebooks and think of at least one idea in each of the PMI columns.

5 Ask everyone to tell their ideas to a partner. If they hear a good idea, they should add it into one of their own PMI columns.

6 Bring the class together and ask for examples from each of the columns.

7 Ask students to note how a PMI analysis can change an instant, gut reaction about a topic into a broader, more considered view.

Follow on
As homework or in a later class, ask students to do a PMI on an idea they have met recently.

Comment
There are a great many kinds of brainstorming besides the 'PMI'. Edward de Bono's *CORT Thinking* (1986), a programme for teaching thinking as a basic skill, is an excellent compendium of examples.

Tessa Woodward

9.9 Great art debate

Age	15 and up
Level	Upper-intermediate–Advanced
Time	30 minutes
Focus	Creating and presenting an argument, expressing a point of view
Material	Reproductions of paintings, as described below, no materials for the Variation

Preparation

The class will be divided into pairs, and each pair needs two colour painting reproductions both of which show the same sort of subject but are of different styles. For example, one pair of reproductions might be a Constable cornfield and the other a Van Gogh cornfield, or one a Dutch still life of kitchen utensils and the other a Ben Nicholson painting of pots and pans. Note that you do not need different paintings for each pair of students (although this will work too). For instance, in a class of 20 it is sufficient to have ten copies of the same Constable and ten copies of the same Van Gogh.

Procedure

1 Show the class one pair of pictures. Elicit some things they like and do not like about each, and list these on the board, plus reasons.

2 Split the class into two halves (A and B) and ask students, within each half, to get into pairs. In each half, number the pairs 1, 2, 3 and so on. Thus, in Group A there will be Pairs A1, A2 and so on and in Group B there will be Pairs B1, B2, etc. Pairs with the same numbers (e.g. A1 and B1) must *not* sit near each other.

3 Give pairs with the same numbers the same pair of pictures. For example, both Pair A1 and Pair B1 get the same Constable and Van Gogh reproductions.

4 Give the pairs different instructions:
   - Tell Pair A1 that they are going to argue that the Constable picture is much better than the Van Gogh.
   - Tell Pair B1 that they are going to argue that the Van Gogh picture is much better than the Constable. Stress to them that each pair should give *concrete* reasons why the one picture is better than the other. And add that they should argue as instructed even if they actually think differently.
   Then allow time for everyone to prepare their arguments.

5 Options:
   - Put the pairs together (e.g. A1 with B1) to debate their cases.

- Set up a situation where the two pairs (e.g. A1 and B1) present their cases to the whole class or to some other pairs, who are also allowed to join in the discussion.

Follow on

The students each write a composition which reflects their *real* opinion. Ask them to include all the relevant points that they have heard, both pro and con. A simple structure for such a composition is as follows: (1) brief introduction, (2) a summary of the points for the opposing opinion, (3) a summary of the points for the side you believe in, including arguments against the previous opposing points, (4) a brief conclusion.

Variation

- Elicit opinions about a 'this versus that' topic such as 'Winter is better than summer versus summer is better than winter'. Do this as in Step 1.
- Divide the class in half, with an equal number of pairs in each half. (Make one or two threesomes if necessary.)
- Tell half your pairs that they will argue one way (e.g. winter is better than summer) while the other half argue the opposite.
- Give them time to prepare their arguments.
- Form groups of four by putting 'winter pairs' and 'summer pairs' together and tell the pairs to present their arguments to each other, challenging, objecting, defending and replying as necessary in order to advance their side.

'This versus that' topics

- winter versus summer
- living in the country versus living in town
- 4×4 cars versus saloon cars
- cars versus motorbikes
- fast food versus home-cooked food
- American movies versus our country's movies
- effective border control versus having no borders at all
- living in a house versus living in a caravan (mobile home)
- buying famous brand goods versus buying other brands or 'no logo' goods
- putting mentally ill people in asylums versus caring for them 'in the community'

© CAMBRIDGE UNIVERSITY PRESS 2004

David A. Hill

9.10 Research notes

Age	12 and up
Level	Intermediate–Advanced
Time	Extends over two or more lessons
Focus	Scanning or listening for relevant information, use of a variety of resources, making and organising notes (e.g. into pro and con points), mental flexibility, finding the general in the particular. This activity acts as preparation for a discussion or debate such as 'Single switch debating' (p. 214).
Material	Class sets of one or more written resources

Preparation

1 In a previous lesson help your class choose a topic of interest to them, e.g. 'friendship' or 'relationships', adding that they will be debating this topic later on.

2 Find and prepare a resource relating to the topic, e.g. article, short story, cassette-recorded interview.

Procedure

LESSON 1

1 Remind your class of the topic they have chosen to examine, but add that at the moment they need not worry about which side of the topic they will be supporting. Explain that over the coming lessons you will be giving them some resources and that they will as well be finding their own resources and making notes on two or three different aspects of the topic: for instance, if the topic is 'friendship', they might collect ideas on 'things that can go right in a friendship', 'things that can go wrong' and 'interesting facts about friendship'. (This echoes the PMI structure of 9.8.)

2 Explain that the resources can include: their memories of personal experience; reports, conversations and interviews that they listen to; materials that they read such as newspaper and magazine articles (including personal problems columns), Internet websites and advertisements; and TV programmes.

3 Tell the class that you are going to start with personal experience and ask them to create three different sections in their notebooks for it: one entitled *Friendship: things that can go right*, a second entitled *Friendship: things that can go wrong* and a third headed *Friendship: interesting facts*.

4   Ask students to suggest ideas for each of the three different sections
    without naming names or giving away personal information. A student
    might say, for example, *Friends can make you happy when you feel sad.* If
    a student starts to say something like *My friend Lisa really helped me the
    other day when I felt sad*, gently stop her, confirming the content of what
    she said by saying, for instance, *I'm really happy about that* and then try
    to help the student to see the *general point* in what she has said. For
    example, *Friends make you feel happy when you are sad.* Work in this
    way with all the contributions, helping the students to see the general in
    the particular.

5   When the class has written down several points for each of the three
    sections, hand out a different kind of resource such as a newspaper article
    or short story relating to the same topic.

6   Ask students to read it for homework, find information relevant to the
    topic and write it, in note form, in the appropriate sections of their
    notebooks.

LESSON 2

7   Put students into groups of three and ask them to pool their ideas and so
    add more information into their notebooks.

8   Bring the class together and ask what has been found out. If necessary,
    help students to see other points in the resource.

9   For homework, ask students each to discuss the topic with friends or
    family in their mother tongue in as much personal detail as they wish, but
    again the idea is to bring back to class at least one new *general* point
    which could be added to any of the three sections in their notebooks.

Follow on

- Tackle a topic such as 'Human cloning: should it be banned in our
  country?' In this case, among other things, students need to find out what
  it is, how far cloning has advanced in practice, whether it has already
  been banned, who is against it and why, who is for it and why, whether
  there are any figures on its cost per 'treatment' in different countries. One
  way of proceeding is to assign different questions to different student
  teams and, after briefing, turn them loose on the Internet. The briefing
  can include the following:
  - Elicit from the class what they know about search engines and how to
    use them.
  - Ask how they have done research in classes on other subjects.

- – In particular, elicit what they know about finding information on serious topics, e.g. find out who has visited the site of an on-line newspaper or news channel.
- – Set guidelines for keeping track of sources.
- – Set rules such as: *Print out for later study only what you have already read through and know to be directly relevant. If only part of a document or site is relevant, print out that part only. As much as possible, take notes and do not print out at all.*
  Colleagues in other subjects should be able to give you tips on how to go about all this.
- Do the fourth Variation of 9.2, 'Pro and con presentations' or 9.11, 'Single switch debating'.

Tips
- Step 4: From time to time remind students that they should be able to support a generalisation. For example, if a student says *Friends can help you when you're sad*, ask for an example of how a friend might do this.
- A subscription to www.thepaperboy.com (a few pounds a month) opens up an amazing wealth of indexed newspaper articles from papers all around the world. Another great (free) research site is http://dmoz.org/.

Tessa Woodward

Doing debating

9.11 Single switch debating

Age	13 and up
Level	Intermediate–Advanced
Time	10–15 minutes in lesson 1, most or all of two further lessons
Focus	All basic debating skills
Material	Various materials may need to be consulted outside class

With this activity students begin to draw near the more complex forms of debate that are followed in club debating: parliamentary debating, for instance.

Preparation
Choose a topic which is interesting, has a positive and negative side, allows both sides an equal chance to develop their arguments and is presented in the form of a proposition, e.g. *In this school homework should be abolished.*

(See further examples on p. 217.) If you are serious about starting real debates, you can now call a topic a 'resolution' or a 'motion'.

Procedure

LESSON 1: PRELIMINARY WORK

1   The class look at the motion, e.g. *Students in this school should not be given homework*, and identify the most important terms. For instance, students need to be clear that this motion refers to 'this' school not others and they need to agree on a definition of *homework*.

2   Students gather information by various means and from various sources, e.g. by interviewing people outside class (members of staff, students of different ages, family members), by looking for relevant material on the Internet and by collecting examples of homework of different types. They are to produce categorised notes as in 'Research notes' (9.10). Add that all class members should collect ideas in support of both sides of the motion.

LESSON 2: THE FIRST ROUND OF DEBATES

3   Form an even number of teams of five or six members each. Designate half the teams as 'pro' (i.e. for the motion) and half as 'con' (i.e. against) but add that by the end of the debate, each team will have had a chance to argue both sides of the motion.

4   Each team now has time to prepare and write down the following: (a) a statement of their argument, (b) an explanation of it, (c) support for it (evidence and reasons) and (d) a conclusion. Allow time for this.

5   Each team decides who will present (a), who (b) and so on.

6   Choose one affirmative (pro) and one negative (con) team. They come to the front of the class and sit around two tables so that they can see each other and the rest of the class.

7   The rest of the class get ready to listen to the first debate and note down any arguments they had not thought of before, regardless of which side these arguments support.

8   In turn, the two teams at the front state their cases and then return to their normal seats.

9   Remind all the teams that they will eventually have to argue both sides of the motion. Ask what arguments were made during the first debate. Allow time for these to be written in their notebooks.

10 Repeat Steps 6–9 with two different teams until all teams have had a chance to state their arguments (still for the side you asked them to represent). This is the end of the first round of debates.

LESSON 3: THE SECOND ROUND OF DEBATES

11 Students sit in the same teams as before. This time they will be arguing the other side of the motion. The purpose is not to defeat the other side but to uncover as many arguments as possible around the topic.

12 Students prepare not just their own arguments but also refutation of arguments they expect the other side to make. Again, they choose different people in the team to put forward different parts of their argument, including the refutations.

13 Repeat Steps 6–9 but this time (instead of simply stating their own arguments after each team has spoken) the opposing team has time to politely refute arguments with reasoned evidence.

14 Lead the class in tallying the number of arguments that have come up on each side of the issue and hold a vote on which side won the debate. If there is time, the other teams also debate at the front of the class.

15 Congratulate all the teams on the preparation and speaking.

Follow on

Everyone writes a summary of the points that came up, followed by a statement of their own actual beliefs.

Variation

Once students have got used to choosing and defining topics, brainstorming ideas, preparing one side of a motion, and then doing a single switch, give them practice in double switch debating where they not only argue a different side in the second round but also do so against different opponents. This can be very energising.

Tip

Just before beginning a debate, suggest students note down privately which side they think they will vote for as winner when the debate is over. After the vote has taken place at the end, ask if anyone changed sides as a result of the debate, and why. There always are people who have changed, and their explanation of how they were convinced is an effective affirmation of the power of persuasive, rational argument.

Example resolutions

We believe that*:

- The government was correct to ....
- Space research is a waste of time and money.
- Strict discipline is the best way of raising children.
- Boxing should be banned.
- Mobile phones and beepers should be allowed in class.
- Paparazzi should be banned.
- A four-day school week is in the best interest of students.
- There should be curfews for teenagers.
- There should be lots of surveillance cameras in schools/towns.
- Studying anything written before 1950 is a waste of time.
- The institution of marriage is obsolete.
- Progress is an illusion.
- Law enforcement is biased against the young.
- In a disaster, women and children should be saved first.
- You should be allowed to keep anything you find.
- After their . . . th birthday, students should be paid to attend school.
- Police powers should be extended.
- Teens should have their own credit cards.
- There should be separate schooling for girls and boys.

* The commonest beginnings in formal club and competition debating are: *Be it resolved that . . .* and *This house resolves that . . .*

Acknowledgements

- Thanks to Alina Gutauskiene: a Lithuanian English teacher and world debate coach, adjudicator, trainer and author, for telling me about using debating in schools. For more information about 'structured controversies', both single and double switch, see d'Eon and Prodou (2001). Several of the topics come from Daley and Dahlie (2001).
- The resolutions, with some changes, come from Brian B. Casey's compilation, *A reservoir of resolutions* (formerly on the web but now removed).

Tessa Woodward

For more about debating

There is a wealth of information on the Internet about all aspects of school debating including how to: form a debate club, join up with existing club debating organisations, and coach debaters. Start with Debate Central at http://debate.uvm.edu/.

Of particular relevance to development of sub-skills of debating

3.10 and 3.11 (being fluent when in the spotlight); 3.12 (structuring a presentation); 3.13 (adopting another person's point of view; fielding lots of questions); 3.14 (dealing with a rain of questions); 3.15 (planning and giving presentations to other students); and 5.1 (mind-mapping a text, relevant to doing pre-debate research)

References

Benson, G., J. Chernaik and C. Herbert. 1999. *Poems on the Underground*. Cassell.

Brookes, A. and P. Grundy. 1999. *Beginning to Write*. Cambridge University Press.

Buzan, T. 1995. *The Mind Map Book*. BBC Books.

Byrne, D. and S. Rixon. 1979. *Communication Games*. NFER.

Cowley, S. 2001. *Getting the Buggers to Behave*. Continuum.

Daley, P. and M. Dahlie. 2001. *50 Debate Prompts for Kids*. Scholastic Professional Books.

Davis, P. and M. Rinvolucri. 1988. *Dictation*. Cambridge University Press.

de Bono, E. 1986. *CORT Thinking*. Oxford: Pergamon Press.

d'Eon, M. and P. Prodou. 2001. 'An innovative modification to structured controversy'. *Innovations in Education and Teaching International*. 38/3. SEDA (Staff and Educational Development Association).

Gathercoal, F. 1993. *Judicious Disclipine*. Caddo Gap Press.

Grinder, M. and B. Doone. 1991. (2nd edn.) *Righting the Educational Conveyor Belt*. Metamorphous Press.

Hess, N. 2002. *Large Classes*. Cambridge University Press.

Holme, R. 1991. *Talking Texts*. Longman.

Holmes, V. L. and M. R. Moulton. 2001. *Writing Simple Poems*. Cambridge University Press.

Hulstijn, J. H. 2001. 'Intentional and incidental second language vocabulary learning'. In Robinson, P., ed., *Cognition and Second Language Instruction*. Cambridge University Press: 258–86.

Johnson, D. W. and R. T. Johnson. 1996. 'Conflict resolution and peer mediation programs in elementary and secondary schools: a review of the research'. *Review of Educational Research*. vol 66/4: 459–506.

Laufer, B. 1997. 'What's in a word that makes it hard or easy: Some intra-lexical factors that affect the learning of words'. In Schmitt, N. and M. McCarthy, eds, *Vocabulary; Description, Acquisition and Pedagogy* (pp. 140–155). Cambridge University Press.

Lindstromberg, S., ed. 1990. *The Recipe Book*. Longman.

Lindstromberg, S., ed. 1997. *The Standby Book*. Cambridge University Press.

Lindstromberg, S. 1997. *English Prepositions Explained.* John Benjamins.

Medgyes, P. 2002. *Laughing Matters.* Cambridge University Press.

Rinvolucri, M. 1993. 'Teacher role play to attack prejudice' in *Modern English Teacher* vol 2/4 pp. 38–9.

Rost, M. 1991. *Listening in Action.* Prentice-Hall.

Swift, E. 2000. 'EFL and conflict resolution: what a combo!!!' in *The Teacher Trainer*, vol 14/2: 20–23.

Williams, W. C. 1976. *Selected Works.* Penguin.

Woodward, T. 2001. *Planning Lessons and Courses.* Cambridge University Press.

Index

Index

Index

CAMBRIDGE
LEARNER'S
DICTIONARY

New Edition

• Fully updated!
• Easy to use
• CD-ROM with sound and thesaurus

Dictionaries for exam success

CD-ROM INSIDE

CAMBRIDGE
UNIVERSITY PRESS

for Windows®
95/98/NT4/2000/ME/XP

A brand new edition makes learning English even easier.
And the whole dictionary is available on CD-ROM, with our UNIQUE SMART thesaurus.
Paperback 0 521 54380 0
Paperback with CD-ROM for Windows 0 521 54381 9
Network CD-ROM (30 users) 0 521 54502 1